Economics SL&HL
FOR THE IB DIPLOMA
Practice Questions for Papers 1 & 2

George Graves

PEAK

Published by:
Peak Study Resources Ltd
1 & 3 Kings Meadow
Oxford OX2 0DP
UK

www.peakib.com

Economics SL&HL Practice Questions for Papers 1 & 2: Study & Revision Guide for the IB Diploma

ISBN 978-1-913433-34-5

© George Graves 2022

George Graves has asserted his right under the Copyright, Design and Patents Act 1988 to be identified as the author of this work.

All rights reserved. No part of this publication may be reproduced, stored in a retrieval system, or transmitted in any form or by any means, without the prior permission of the publishers.

*PHOTOCOPYING ANY PAGES FROM THIS PUBLICATION,
EXCEPT UNDER LICENCE, IS PROHIBITED*

Peak Study & Revision Guides for the IB Diploma have been developed independently of the International Baccalaureate Organization (IBO). 'International Baccalaureate' and 'IB' are registered trademarks of the IBO.

Books may be ordered directly from the publisher (see www.peakib.com) and through online or local booksellers. For enquiries regarding titles, availability or retailers, please email books@peakib.com or use the form at www.peakib.com/contact.

Printed and bound in the UK
CPI Group (UK) Ltd, Croydon CR0 4YY
www.cpibooks.co.uk

Cover image: Adobe Stock

The purpose of this guide is to assist you with your preparation for the final IB Economics exam. It accompanies my study guides for Economics at standard and higher level, and therefore does not contain the topic review that those books provide. Instead, it is designed to provide practice undertaking exam-style questions on a range of topics, for which I provide model answers and commentary where helpful.

This guide is structured with an introduction to the examination paper, containing important information about structure and mark allocations, followed by a chapter of exam-style practice questions.

Each question is immediately followed by an answer, see my comments in the introductory chapters for the marks these answers would be expected to receive.

Where I have included commentary and advice, this is in highlighted sections marked with the icon shown on the right. This icon should be familiar to students using my other Economics books or any of the other Peak study guides for the IB.

You can also find some additional resources on the Peak website relating to both IB Economics and practical study advice – see the back cover for the details and a QR code link.

Finally, as you approach the end of your IB Diploma Programme, I wish you all the best with your studies and beyond.

George Graves

Contents

Chapter 1: Introduction to paper 1 1
1.1   General points   1
1.2   A word of caution   2
1.3   Assessment criteria   3

Chapter 2: Paper 1 practice questions 5
2.1   Unit 2 Microeconomics   5
2.2   Unit 3 Macroeconomics   23
2.3   Unit 4 Global Economics   37

Chapter 3: Introduction to paper 2 50
3.1   General points   50
3.2   Assessment criteria   51

Chapter 4: Paper 2 practice questions 52

Chapter 1: Introduction to paper 1

For the new syllabus in Economics for first examination in May 2022, paper 1 has undergone three significant changes. It is still an extended response (long essay) question paper with a part (a) for 10 marks and a part (b) for 15 marks *but*:

- you are now required to do only **one** question out of a choice of **three**;
- the time allowed is 1 hour and 15 minutes;
- the questions may be taken from all four units of the syllabus.

The format is the same for both HL and SL, the only difference being that for SL paper 1 accounts for 30% of the total marks for the subject whereas for HL it accounts for 20% of the total marks. Since the HL syllabus includes more topics some questions will only be set on the HL paper, but for common topics the same question may be set on both the HL and SL paper.

1.1 General points

In the exam, you will have five minutes of **reading time.** This time should be used to read each question carefully in order to decide which question should be attempted. Mentally run through the definitions of terms and the relevant diagrams that are required and select the question which you feel best able to analyse. Give greater emphasis to part (b) of the question as this carries more weight in terms of marks.

Part (a) will usually ask you to explain two economic concepts/reasons/causes/factors and you should confine your answer to this explanation. No discussion or evaluation is necessary in part (a). You should identify all the economic terms included in the question and give a clear and concise definition of each term. Your explanation will usually be assisted by the inclusion of one or more relevant diagrams and you must be careful to make sure that the diagrams are *clear, fully labelled* and *explained* so that they relate to the actual question. Diagrams do not require a title but should be numbered and referred to by number. This is especially important because you might want to refer to a diagram from part (a) in your answer to part (b) and you can only do this if you have numbered the diagram. You are not expected to duplicate diagrams or definitions in part (b) that you have used in part (a).

Part (b) will usually be related to part (a) but will often require a discussion or evaluation of a policy or a market situation. According to the sample exam papers provided by the IB it appears that all part (b) questions will begin as follows: '*Using real-world examples, discuss/evaluate...*' To do this effectively it is necessary to establish the criteria which you will apply. Possible criteria include efficiency, desirability, effectiveness, advantages/ disadvantages (costs/benefits), effects on different groups, differences between time periods and the relative importance of the points that have been identified. As far as possible these criteria should be related to effects on stakeholders while using the real-world examples to illustrate. At least one of these criteria needs to be applied in order to secure the marks set aside for evaluation or discussion. Many questions are quite specific and require a specific answer which you should attempt to provide. If, for example, the question asks, "*To what extent...?*" you should address this in your conclusion with a phrase such as: to a large extent or to a limited extent. Similarly, if the question asks you to discuss the effectiveness of a policy you need to include this in your conclusion with a statement which assesses the overall effectiveness. Hopefully, these points will become clearer in the section which presents answers to specific questions.

1.2   A word of caution

The fact that the time allowed for writing each extended response question has been increased from 45 minutes to 1 hour and 15 minutes partly reflects a realisation that for many students 45 minutes is insufficient time to produce an effective answer.

However, there will also be an expectation that the better students will be able to produce more detailed and significantly longer answers, especially for the part (b) questions. It would be sensible to allocate the time between part (a) and part (b) according to the marks for each section. This works out to 30 minutes for part (a) and 45 minutes for part (b). However, it is likely that a good answer to part (a) could be provided in a bit less than 30 minutes which could leave a few extra minutes for providing a longer and more detailed analysis for part (b).

For students who have an excellent command of English and an extensive training in writing essays the time allowed will enable them to write many pages of relevant material in their answers. For many students though, finding enough to write will be a serious challenge. The key to solving this challenge is two-fold:

- a deeper understanding and knowledge of the topics is required, and
- it is imperative that at least *two* real-world examples can be identified and explained clearly and appropriately in order to support the discussion or evaluation.

This means that it is not enough to simply state the example. The real-world examples need to be explained in detail with their relevance to the question clearly presented and emphasised. Hopefully, the suggested answers to the selected questions will illustrate how this can be done in order to secure the maximum marks possible. Your knowledge of real-world examples is therefore crucial to your ability to perform well on this paper and it should be a major guide to which question you select to answer. *Do not* select a question for which you have no knowledge of real-life examples that are relevant.

Conventional wisdom for essay writing states that you should begin with a plan which sets out the structure of the essay and the main points to include. Ideally this should be written down as a rough outline. This should prevent aimless rambling in search of relevant points. It also concentrates the mind on the question and helps to identify and remember the main points which should be included in the essay.

Finally, you should note that with the use of e-marking for economics exams it is not possible to differentiate colours, as everything is viewed by the examiner in black and white. Therefore, you should not use coloured pencils or pens in your diagrams.

HAVE A PLAN

Unfortunately, few students have developed the good habit of writing a plan, but I would urge you to at least make a mental plan before you start writing down your answer. A good idea might be to make a note of the real-world examples that you will be using.

1. INTRODUCTION TO PAPER 1

1.3 Assessment criteria

The following represent the Assessment Criteria and Mark Bands that the IB examiners will apply to paper 1 questions (as presented in the sample exam papers).

Part (a) 10 marks

Marks	Level descriptor
0	• The work does not reach a standard described by the descriptors below.
1–2	• The response indicates little understanding of the specific demands of the question. • Economic theory is stated but it is not relevant. • Economic terms are stated but they are not relevant.
3–4	• The response indicates some understanding of the specific demands of the question. • Relevant economic theory is described. • Some relevant economic terms are included.
5–6	• The response indicates understanding of the specific demands of the question, but these demands are only partially addressed. • Relevant economic theory is partly explained. • Some relevant economic terms are used appropriately. • Where appropriate, relevant diagram(s) are included.
7–8	• The specific demands of the question are understood and addressed. • Relevant economic theory is explained. • Relevant economic terms are used mostly appropriately. • Where appropriate, relevant diagram(s) are included and explained.
9–10	• The specific demands of the question are understood and addressed. • Relevant economic theory is fully explained. • Relevant economic terms are used appropriately throughout the response. • Where appropriate, relevant diagram(s) are included and fully explained.

ECONOMICS SL&HL: PRACTICE QUESTIONS FOR PAPERS 1 & 2

Part (b) 15 marks

Marks	Level descriptor
0	• The work does not reach a standard described by the descriptors below.
1–3	• The response indicates little understanding of the specific demands of the question. • Economic theory is stated but it is not relevant. • Economic terms are stated but they are not relevant. • The response contains no evidence of synthesis or evaluation. • A real-world example(s) is identified but it is irrelevant.
4–6	• The response indicates some understanding of the specific demands of the question. • Relevant economic theory is described. • Some relevant economic terms are included. • The response contains evidence of superficial synthesis or evaluation. • A relevant real-world example(s) is identified.
7–9	• The response indicates understanding of the specific demands of the question, but these demands are only partially addressed. • Relevant economic theory is partly explained. • Some relevant economic terms are used appropriately. • Where appropriate, relevant diagram(s) are included. • The response contains evidence of appropriate synthesis or evaluation but lacks balance. • A relevant real-world example(s) is identified and partly developed in the context of the question.
10–12	• The specific demands of the question are understood and addressed. • Relevant economic theory is explained. • Relevant economic terms are used mostly appropriately. • Where appropriate, relevant diagram(s) are included and explained. • The response contains evidence of appropriate synthesis or evaluation that is mostly balanced. • A relevant real-world example(s) is identified and developed in the context of the question.
13–15	• The specific demands of the question are understood and addressed. • Relevant economic theory is fully explained. • Relevant economic terms are used appropriately throughout the response. • Where appropriate, relevant diagram(s) are included and fully explained. • The response contains evidence of effective and balanced synthesis or evaluation. • A relevant real-world example(s) is identified and fully developed to support the argument.

From the above descriptors it is important to note that in order to have a chance of gaining the highest mark bands, theory, diagrams and relevant real-world examples must be *fully* developed and explained. It remains to be seen how the 'fullness' of an explanation will be interpreted by the examiners.

Chapter 2: Paper 1 practice questions

Although the syllabus suggests that questions may be set on all four sections of the syllabus, it is unlikely that many, if any, will be set on Unit 1: Introduction to Economics (for which only 10 hours of teaching time is recommended).

The greatest likelihood is therefore that the three questions will be set on the remaining sections of the syllabus, namely:

- Unit 2 Microeconomics
- Unit 3 Macroeconomics
- Unit 4 The Global Economy.

The expectation will be for one question to be set on each of these three units as this is the impression given by the sample HL and SL exams available at the time of writing this guide, and this section contains four representative questions with answers for each.

2.1 Unit 2 Microeconomics

Question 1

(a) Explain two reasons why a government might impose a price floor (minimum price) in a market. [10 marks]

(b) Using real-world examples, discuss the consequences of a price floor on stakeholders. [15 marks]

Before proceeding with an answer to this question I will identify some of the points mentioned in the introduction regarding how best to go about answering such questions.

Part (a): The first task here is to provide a clear definition of a price floor (minimum price). Next you should identify and explain two possible reasons or motives for this form of intervention in a market. Finally, you should consider the need for an appropriate diagram to illustrate the effect of the imposition of a price floor. Without a clear fully labelled and fully explained diagram it is most unlikely that you would score more than 4 marks for this question. If these three tasks are performed well it should be possible to achieve a mark in the highest band though bear in mind that past experience indicates that examiners are reluctant to give full marks for extended response questions. A mark of 8 or 9 out of 10 is probably the most that you can hope for. Note that the question does not specify the type of market so the analysis can include the labour market and the imposition of a minimum wage.

Part (b): Here it would be sensible to begin with a general introduction which identifies the range of stakeholders who will be affected. By selecting appropriate examples, it is easier to discuss the consequences of where such policies have been applied. A good starting point would be to identify examples of where price floors have been used and to evaluate the effectiveness of such policies. Then consider some alternative policies that have been applied and evaluate these. Finally, an overall evaluation is required that will consider which policies appear to have produced the best results according to the real-world examples that have been used and the relative effects on the relevant stakeholders.

Answer

1 (a) A price floor, or minimum price, is an example of a price control imposed on the market for a good by the government. It makes it illegal to sell the good at a lower price than the specified minimum but will only affect the market if it is imposed above the existing market price. The decision to intervene in a market suggests that the free market outcome is undesirable in certain respects and that these failures can be resolved by imposing a minimum price.

There are two main reasons why the government might choose to select this form of intervention. The first is to ensure that the suppliers of the product are guaranteed a price which is sufficient to cover their costs and provide them with a satisfactory income. The implication here is that the market price would be too low to sustain production at a desired level.

The second reason might be to introduce a greater degree of stability in a market which suffers from a high degree of volatility observed through frequent price fluctuations over time.

(An alternative reason could be to ensure that workers receive a living wage if a minimum wage is selected as the policy.)

The markets where minimum prices have typically been imposed are usually in the agricultural commodity sector which is characterised by a high degree of price instability in response to frequent changes in market conditions, especially on the supply side. Low and unstable prices can lead to extreme hardship for producers and their families and can lead producers to abandon their crop cultivation and migrate to urban centres or to foreign countries. A guaranteed minimum price can to some extent reduce these risks and allow the producers to continue operating in the market. Examples of markets affected by low or unstable prices include coffee, cocoa, cotton and sugar. The effect of a price floor imposed on such markets is illustrated in diagram 1.

Diagram 1 shows that in a free market the price will be at P_e and quantity at Q_e. If this price is considered to be too low to sustain production and provide a satisfactory income for producers, the government might decide to impose a minimum price in the form of a guaranteed price at P_g. As long as this guaranteed price remains above the equilibrium price it will lead to a surplus of the product because supply will increase to Q_2 while demand will decrease to Q_1. The surplus Q_1Q_2 will have to be removed from the market otherwise price will fall back to the equilibrium. This is normally achieved by the government, or the authority, that administers the guaranteed price buying the surplus at the guaranteed price. The surplus might be stored if the product is not perishable or disposed of in some other way.

2. PAPER 1 PRACTICE QUESTIONS

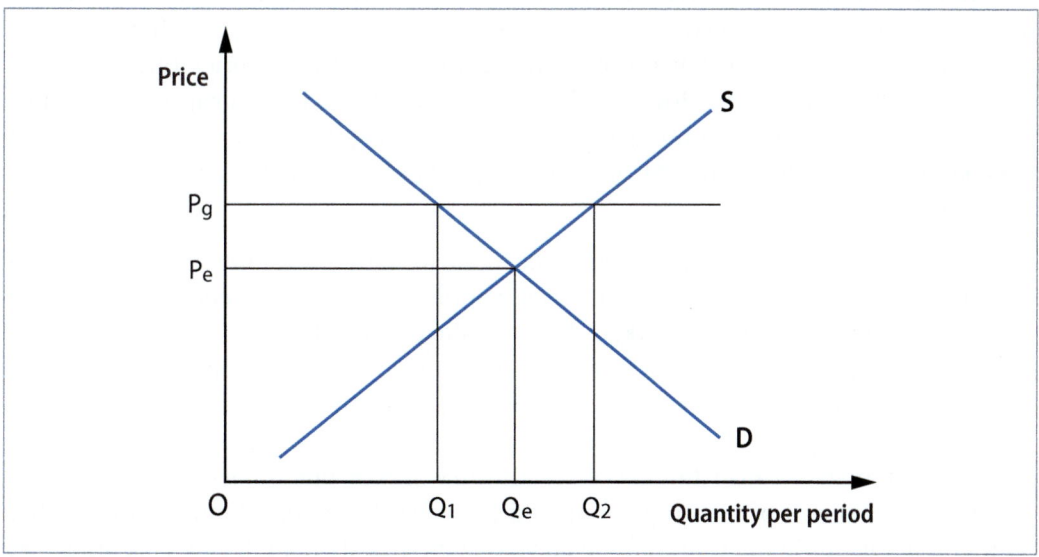

Diagram 1

Note that in the case that you decide to analyse the imposition of a minimum wage the diagram will be labelled as wage rate instead of price and Quantity of labour per period. Also, the minimum price will be labelled W_m. The surplus Q_1Q_2 will now represent workers who are willing to work but who are unable to find work and therefore constitute an increase in unemployment.)

You should resist the temptation to include some discussion or evaluation in part (a). This should be left for part (b) where it is a requirement and will score marks. Including an evaluation point in part (a) will not score any marks.

---

1 (b) The stakeholders that will be affected by the imposition of a minimum price (defined in part (a)) are consumers, producers and the government. Some of these consequences can be observed from diagram 1 in part (a). Specifically, for the government a major consequence will be the cost of the policy if the minimum price is imposed in the market for a product. In diagram 1 this cost will be the excess supply Q_1Q_2 that will have to be bought at the guaranteed price P_g. It is necessary to remove the excess supply from the market otherwise the guaranteed price could not be maintained. Having bought the surplus, the government then must decide what to do with it. One possibility is to store it, but this will involve additional storage costs and can only be applied to products that can be stored such as coffee or cocoa. Keeping stocks of such commodities could be used as a buffer to stabilise prices in the future if there was a sudden decrease in the market supply. In this case the stocks could be released on to the market and sold at the guaranteed price thus recovering some of the costs. However, real-world examples of such minimum price interventions suggest that the most likely result is a build up of excessive stocks over time that eventually need to be disposed of. The Common Agricultural Policy (CAP) that was employed by the EU between 1960 and 1992 provided guaranteed prices for a wide range of agricultural products such as wheat, sugar, butter, wine and milk. The result of this policy was that huge surpluses of these products built up and in order to reduce storage problems the EU encouraged exports with the use of export subsidies. This involved additional costs and also had a major negative impact on other countries as the subsidised EU products undermined domestic producers in the countries that received the subsidised exports. During the 1990s the high cost of CAP and the market distortions that it encouraged led to increasing criticism from both member countries and non-EU countries so that the guaranteed prices for many agricultural products were gradually phased out. However, for some products such as sugar, price support and export subsidies have continued to facilitate dumping which seriously impacts on cheaper foreign producers like Mozambique who cannot export their sugar at genuine market prices.

In the case of a price floor or minimum price in the form of a minimum wage, the cost to the government is not direct since the excess supply represents workers who will not be bought and removed from the market. However, since some of these workers will now be unemployed, the government will face some additional costs in unemployment benefits as well as some loss in tax revenues from less income tax and lower indirect tax receipts because the unemployed will spend less that wage earners. The extent of these costs is difficult to estimate because the effect of minimum wages on unemployment is uncertain. An extensive amount of research conducted in the USA has found little evidence that increases in the minimum wage have in fact led to increased unemployment as predicted by economic theory. According to a National Employment Law Project study in 2016, a review of seven decades of historical data found no correlation between minimum wage increases and employment levels. There are several possible reasons for this result that appears to contradict economic theory such as the fact that the minimum wage increase reduces labour turnover, the cost of which is more than the additional wage cost. Another possibility is that it removes the need for employers to bargain wages individually with workers and creates a level playing field for employers as they know that their competitors are also paying the same wage. If this is indeed the case, then minimum wages do not impose any significant cost and since the lowest paid workers and their families benefit there is likely to be a net gain for the economy. It is also possible that the increase in wages will generate more spending and demand in the economy which will benefit producers through increased sales.

Consumers are the least likely to benefit from minimum or guaranteed prices as these prices will invariably be higher than the market price leading consumers to pay higher prices and consume lower quantities than if the market price prevailed. In addition, consumers as taxpayers will be paying the cost of the policy which will also represent an opportunity cost because the amount spent by the government could have been spent on something else such as health care. Higher prices also mean a reduction in consumer surplus which will be transferred to producers.

Producers will be the net gainers from the policy as they will receive a stable guaranteed price and income. Diagram 1 in (a) shows that producer's revenue will increase from $OP_e \times OQ_e$ to $OP_g \times OQ_2$. In addition, producers will have less incentive to become more efficient and to cut costs or explore better production methods. In fact, the incentive they now have is to produce as much as possible since they have a guaranteed buyer for any surplus. These benefits, however, will only be enjoyed by the producers of the products receiving the guaranteed prices. As more scarce resources are channelled to producing these products, fewer resources are available to other producers who will now face higher costs as a result. Some farmers will switch production to goods receiving the guaranteed prices and the reduction in the supply of the goods that they switch from will cause the prices of these goods to increase. Consumers will therefore face higher prices for a wide range of agricultural products as a result of any extensive guaranteed price policy.

Although some domestic producers will benefit from the policy, foreign producers might suffer depending on how the government decides to deal with the surplus of goods that is created. If they are exported with the aid of subsidies as in the case of sugar, producers in sugar producing countries such as Mozambique will be squeezed out of world markets and prevented from exporting their sugar. Sometimes well-intentioned governments decide to send the surplus products as free food aid to poor countries. Such decisions, however, can have a devastating effect on producers in those countries since with free food available people will not be buying locally produced food. Local farmers will be forced out of business and unable to buy seeds for planting future crops leading to future food shortages and increased poverty.

Overall, it appears to be the case that more stakeholders will lose than those who gain from such a policy except possibly in the case of a minimum wage where evidence suggests that there might not be a negative effect on employment. In the case of price floors on agricultural goods the costs most definitely outweigh the benefits and it is not surprising that the policy of guaranteed prices for farmers has been gradually phased out and replaced by simpler and more direct methods of support for farmers. A more sensible and less costly policy would be to allow the free market to allocate resources efficiently through signals and incentives and provide low income farmers with income supplements in the years that prices are low.

The answer provided above is by no means the only acceptable response to this question. What is important is that it includes the essential elements required by the question, namely:

- clear definition and understanding of the nature of price floors;
- a diagram showing the effects of a price floor;
- an indication of the affected stakeholders;
- real-world examples to illustrate the operation and effects of actual price floor interventions; and
- an overall assessment of the effects on stakeholders.

It would be perfectly acceptable to use a minimum wage diagram or a more detailed diagram linking the price floor to a buffer-stock scheme, though this is not specifically included in the new syllabus. Alternatively, hypothetical prices and quantities could be used on the diagram in order to provide actual figures for the cost to the government and the increase in revenue to producers. Though useful, such detail is not specifically required. Finally, different real-world examples could be used which might lead to different conclusions regarding effects on stakeholders.

ECONOMICS SL&HL: PRACTICE QUESTIONS FOR PAPERS 1 & 2

Question 2

(a) Explain two possible causes of an increase in the price of bread. [10 marks]

(b) Using real-world examples, discuss the consequences on stakeholders of subsidies to producers of basic food. [15 marks]

This is a question that could appear on either the HL or SL paper and appears to be a straightforward question that most students would feel comfortable in answering. The challenge here is to go beyond the most obvious and basic points and to come up with something a bit more original and interesting in order to gain some additional marks.

Answer

2(a) In a free market the price of bread will be determined by the market forces of supply and demand. The market for bread will be in equilibrium when price is established at the level which equates quantity demanded with quantity supplied. For this price to increase requires that either demand increases (shifts to the right) or that supply decreases (shifts to the left). Such shifts in demand or supply can be caused by any change in the conditions of demand or supply. Apart from price which determines the quantity demanded, the demand for a product such as bread will be influenced by a variety of factors, the most important of which are income, tastes and preferences of consumers and the prices of related goods such as substitutes or complements. A change in any of these factors will cause the demand to shift leading to a new equilibrium price. If bread is a normal good an increase in demand could be caused by an increase in the incomes of consumers and ceteris paribus, this will lead to an increase in price as shown in diagram 1.

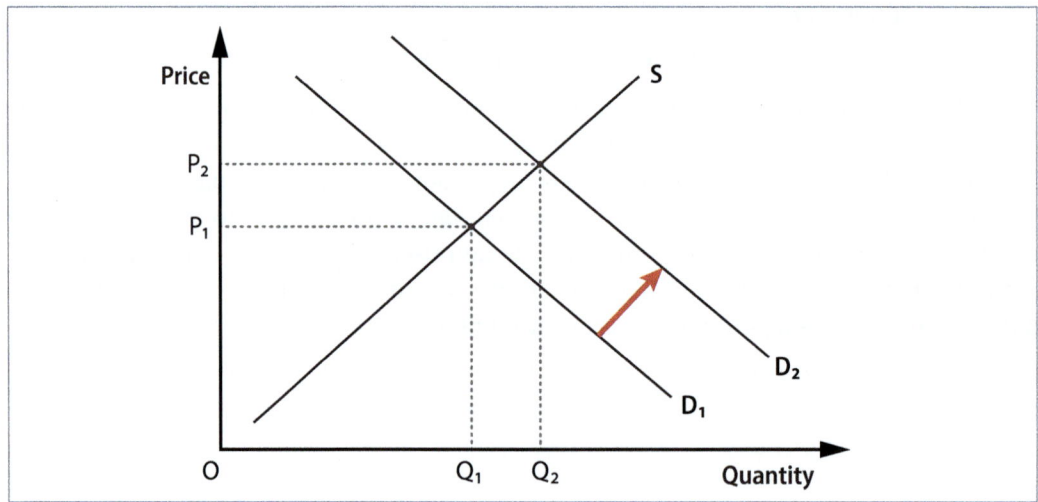

Diagram 1

The increase in income causes demand to shift to D_2 leading to an increase in price from OP_1 to OP_2 and an increase in quantity traded from OQ_1 to OQ_2. (A similar shift in demand to the right could have been caused by a change in consumer tastes in favour of bread, an increase in the price of a substitute such as rice or a decrease in the price of a complement such as butter, or if bread was an inferior good a fall in consumers' incomes.*)

Similarly, an increase in the price of bread could be caused by a decrease in supply which in turn could be caused by changes in the conditions of supply. The most important of these are the costs of production that bread producers face. For example, an increase in

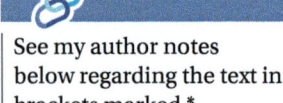

See my author notes below regarding the text in brackets marked *

the price of wheat would raise the production costs for bakers causing supply to shift to the left as shown in diagram 2.

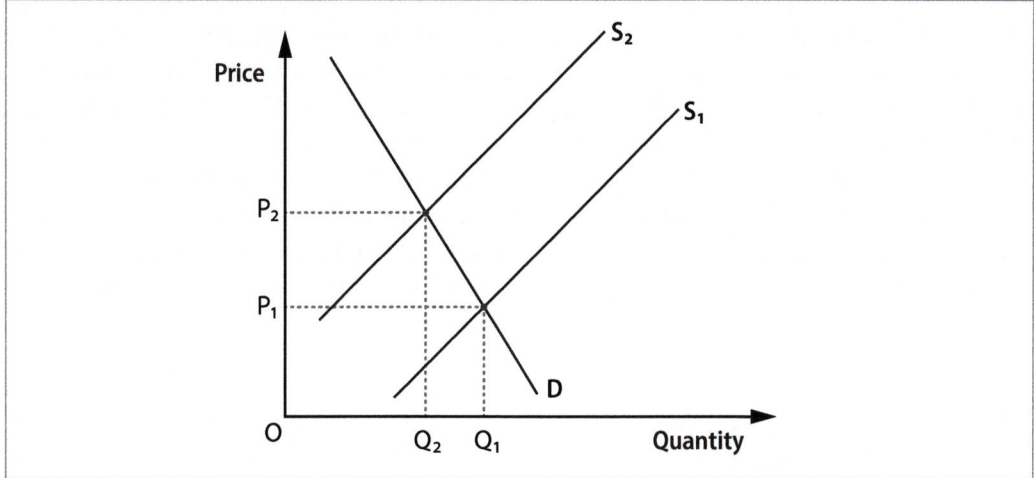

Diagram 2

The increase in production costs causes supply to shift to S_2 and as a result the price of bread increases from P_1 to P_2 and quantity traded falls from Q_1 to Q_2. (Other factors that could cause supply to decrease include other cost of production increases such as rents for bakeries or reduction of subsidies or imposition of taxes on bread.*)

Essentially the question has been answered and virtually all students selecting this question would be able to include the main points included together with the two diagrams. The challenge now is to come up with something extra to make your answer a bit better and to gain one or two additional marks. This involves finding some relevant points that allow you to show off your knowledge.

This could be done by including the two sections in brackets marked*. This is not a requirement of the question but is a good opportunity for showing wider knowledge of possible factors that can cause demand or supply to shift.

An alternative is to show off your knowledge of inferior goods by using the example of a fall in income if bread is an inferior good.

If using the income determinant of demand, you could make a reference to the income elasticity of demand that would determine the extent of the shift in demand.

Another possibility is to consider the price elasticity of supply and demand that would determine the amount of the change in price following the shifts in demand and supply. The more elastic the demand and supply, the smaller the price change for a given shift. This could be included in the diagrams using steep or flat demand and supply functions.

An increase in the price of bread could also be the result of the imposition of a price floor and this could be used as one of your causes which gives you the opportunity of using the price floor diagram as in the previous question. It is unlikely however, that the government would ever impose a minimum price on a product such as bread so I would not recommend using this example.

2 (b) Subsidies represent a payment by the government to producers which lowers their costs of production leading to a decrease in price and an increase in the quantity of the product that is produced and consumed. There are many examples of how subsidies are used by governments to either encourage the production or consumption of products and among the most popular are subsidies granted to the producers of basic food such as bread, rice, various cereals and milk. Such subsidies are very common in low- and middle-income countries, but there are also many examples of such subsidies in high income countries like the USA and the EU. In fact, the EU has one of the largest subsidy programs in the world amounting to $65 billion a year which is over three times the total value of US farm subsidies. Such large expenditures are likely to have a significant impact on the three stakeholder groups of producers, consumers and the government. Some of these effects can be identified from diagram 3 which shows how a subsidy impacts price and output.

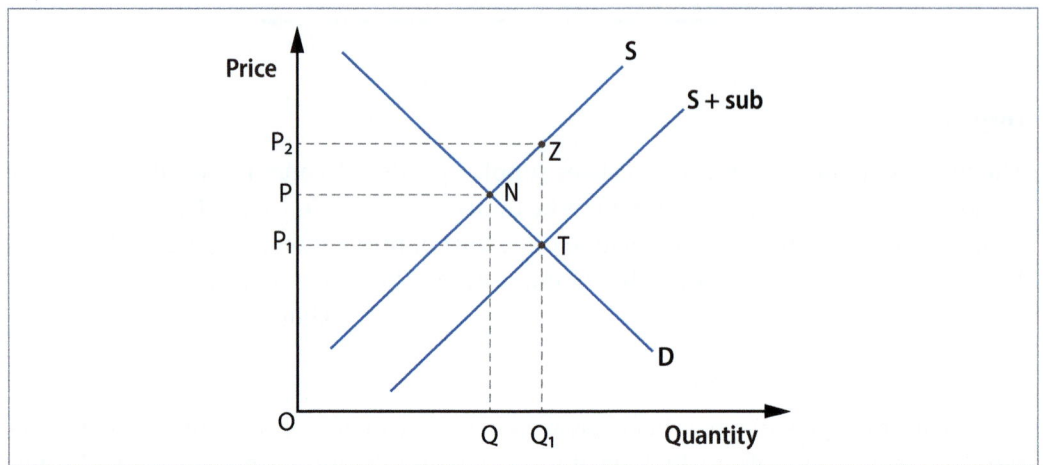

Diagram 3

Assuming a specific subsidy per unit is granted to producers this will reduce production costs by the amount of the unit subsidy causing the supply of the product to shift to the right to S+sub. This leads to a decrease in price to P_1 and an increase in quantity to Q_1. The cost to the government is represented by the unit subsidy × the new quantity Q_1 which is equal to the area P_1P_2ZT. In many countries the cost of food subsidies is considerable and involves a significant opportunity cost. For example, the $65 billion paid in subsidies in the EU could be used for alternative development projects to assist the poorer regions or to provide better health care and education which would generate external benefits. Producers who receive the subsidy gain an increase in revenues from OPNQ to OP_2ZQ_1 while consumers of the subsidised products gain an increase in consumer surplus equal to the area P_1PNT as a result of consuming more at a lower price. Overall, there could be a net welfare gain or loss depending on whether the increase in consumer and producer surplus is greater or smaller than the total cost of the subsidy to the government.

The above represents the general effects of subsidies on broad stakeholder groups, however a comprehensive assessment of the consequences requires a more detailed examination of wider stakeholder sub-groups in conjunction with actual real-world examples of food subsidies. Subsidies, by interfering with the allocative function of the price mechanism, generate artificial signals and incentives, which encourage the production of certain goods at the expense of other alternative food products. Although the producers of the subsidised products will benefit, the producers of substitute food products will face falling demand for their products and consequently falling incomes. It is also necessary to consider what the intention of the subsidy was. The stated aim of food subsidies is usually to guarantee food security and to help protect vulnerable farmers from unstable market conditions, while at the same time ensuring that the basic foods are supplied in large quantities at affordable prices to consumers. The balance between these objectives is likely to be different in different types of economy. In low- and middle-income economies like India and Egypt food subsidies generally aim to benefit consumers whereas in high income countries like the US and EU the emphasis is more on assisting the poorer farmers. However, far from helping poor farmers, the US farm subsidies overwhelmingly assist the largest and wealthiest farmers. It is estimated that the top 10% of farms by size receive over 70% of farm subsidies and that 50 people on the Forbes list of the 400 wealthiest Americans are in receipt of farm subsidies, while over 60% of American farmers receive no subsidies at all. A similar situation exists in the EU where according to an article published in 2019 in the New York Times the bulk of the subsidies (80%) are received by the largest 20% of farmers. In addition, the subsidies are apparently being misused by governments in Hungary, and other Central and Eastern European countries for political purposes and personal enrichment.

Low- and middle-income economies use food subsidies mainly to achieve a higher degree of food security and to ensure affordable prices for basic foods. This is often a very costly policy however, for example in Egypt food subsidies account for around 5% of government spending and 2% of GDP. Undoubtedly, this will have a major impact on the real incomes of the poorest households who spend a large proportion of their income on food. There is, however, some doubt whether basic food subsidies will encourage healthy eating or not. Some studies have shown that by encouraging the consumption of foods that are high in carbohydrates, subsidies are increasingly contributing to the problem of obesity and bad health. Healthy foods tend to be more expensive and the subsidies will lead to an even greater substitution of less healthy for more healthy food.

Overall, it is difficult to assess the benefits of food subsidies for consumers because for some consumers it has the benefit of ensuring adequate food to prevent malnutrition while for others it might encourage increased consumption of unhealthy food. This is especially the case for countries like Egypt and the EU which subsidise sugar. For those consumers who do not buy the subsidised foods there is no benefit because as taxpayers they will be paying taxes which are used to subsidise products that they do not consume and the subsidies will tend to lead to increased prices for non-subsidised food that they do consume. In countries like Egypt and India, the large amounts that are spent on food subsidies face a high opportunity cost because there are many potential alternatives that could have a significant impact on growth and development such as better health care and primary school education.

Producers of the subsidised products will benefit but in some countries it is the large farming companies that will benefit rather than the small and poorer farmers. Any benefits to these producers will be at the expense of producers of non-subsidised food products. Indirectly producers of complementary products to the subsidised goods will also benefit. For example, subsidies given to sugar producers will benefit manufacturers of chocolate and cakes who will face lower production costs. Subsidies to wheat farmers will benefit producers of flour, bread and pasta.

Finally, high subsidies for products in a country can have an impact on foreign producers if the subsidised food is exported. If India gives subsidies to rice farmers and this leads to more rice exports, it could undermine rice production in other countries. Whether the benefits of subsidies for stakeholders outweigh the costs to stakeholders in the long run is debatable and it is certain that the consequences will tend to be mixed and often arbitrary.

ECONOMICS SL&HL: PRACTICE QUESTIONS FOR PAPERS 1 & 2

This part (b) is essentially a fairly straight forward question requiring a basic knowledge of economic theory as applied to subsidies and an accurate diagram from which the effects on stakeholders can be identified. My experience of teaching revision classes is that very few students are able to show the cost to the government on the subsidy diagram so make sure that you are able to do this. Although most students are able to identify the broad stakeholder groups of government, producers and consumers, few will be able to go beyond this and identify subgroups that might be affected differently. It is always important to consider the possibility of producer and consumer subgroups.

The major difficulty, however, is to have a range of real-world examples that can be effectively applied in order to illustrate the consequences for stakeholders. Several have been included here but students are not likely to have such detailed knowledge of subsidies in the real-world. Clearly however, to do well in these questions the student who aspires to securing the highest grades will have to have a good bank of real-world examples to draw from.

Again, the answer provided is by no means a perfect answer or the only possible answer that could be written. There are additional points that could be mentioned such as the importance of both price elasticity and income elasticity of demand and price elasticity of supply for the determination of consequences. Different examples could have been selected possibly leading to different consequences. There is a limit to how much can be written in the time allowed so the aim must always be to answer the question clearly and concisely with appropriate economic analysis and satisfactory examples.

Question 3

(a) Explain two ways a government might respond to the problem of over consumption of unhealthy food. [10 marks]

(b) Using real-world examples, evaluate alternative approaches to limiting the extent of negative consumption externalities. [15 marks]

*This is a typical market failure question which could appear on either the HL or SL paper as it is not related to asymmetric information that is exclusively HL. I have phrased the question in the way that the IB seems to prefer by asking for possible responses rather than **actual** policies which is what the question is **presumably** seeking. I would be interested to know how the IB examiners would **respond** to an answer that identified not doing anything as a possible response to a particular problem.*

Answer

3 (a) The consumption of unhealthy food is generally regarded to have contributed to a variety of potentially serious medical conditions such as obesity and diabetes. What constitutes unhealthy food is not easy to define objectively, but most people would include foods with a high sugar and salt content together with those that have a high content of certain fats and calories. Examples are sugary drinks and many varieties of fast food products and snacks. It is likely that in a free market these products will be over-consumed, meaning that a larger quantity than is socially desirable will be consumed. Such a situation represents a market failure that arises because the private benefit from consumption is greater than the social benefit. This type of market failure can be shown with a negative consumption externality diagram as in diagram 1. Whenever, a transaction between two parties generates a cost to a third party it is described as a negative externality. Diagram 1 shows that in a free market the consumption of unhealthy food will be at Q_m but the socially desirable or optimum level of consumption is at Q_o.

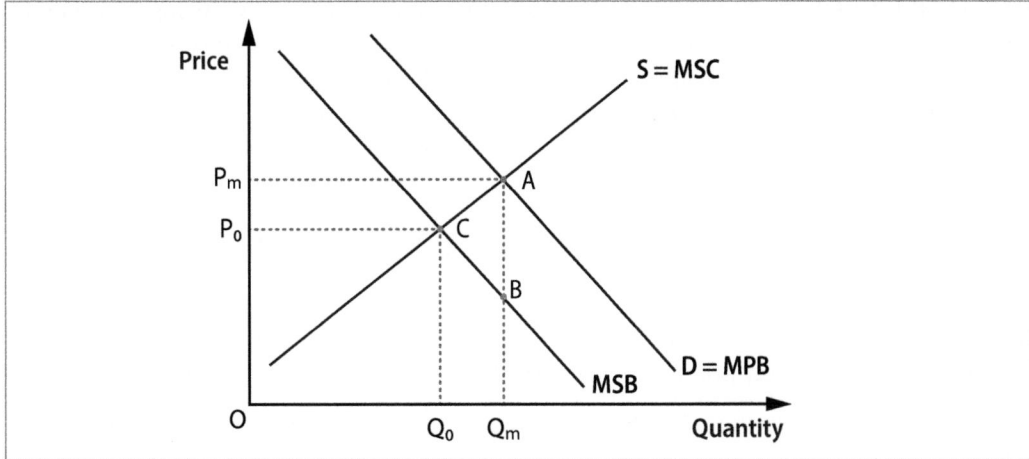

Diagram 1

The free market will equate demand, as represented by the marginal private benefit, with supply as represented by the marginal social cost. The optimum however, is achieved when the marginal social cost is equal to the marginal social benefit which would be at Q_o. There is therefore a market failure of overconsumption equal to Q_oQ_m leading to a welfare or efficiency loss equal to the area ABC.

Assuming that the government response is positive with the aim of reducing or removing the overconsumption there are two main alternative policies that can be applied. One is through rules and regulations and the other is through a market-based solution.

The most direct market-based solution is to reduce the quantity demanded of unhealthy food by increasing its price through the imposition of an indirect tax on the products. For example, a tax on sugary drinks will increase the costs of production by the amount of the tax and cause the supply to shift to the left by this amount.

The effect of this is shown in diagram 2.

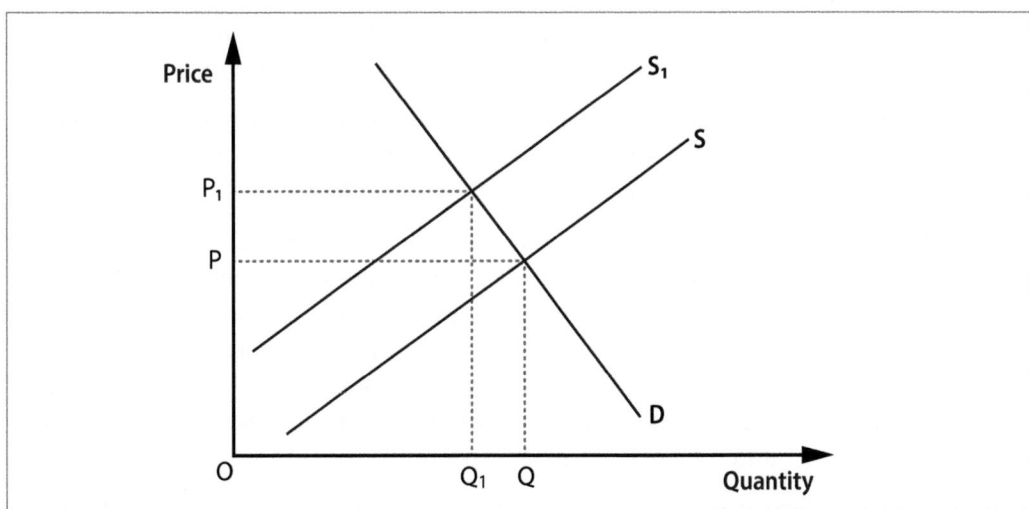

Diagram 2

Supply will shift from S to S_1 and as a result the price will increase from OP to OP_1. The increase in price will lead to a decrease in the quantity consumed from OQ to OQ_1 and the amount of overconsumption will be reduced or even removed.

The alternative policy response is to try to shift the entire demand to the left from MPB towards MSB which could be achieved through the financing of advertising campaigns which highlight the negative health effects of consuming too much sugary and unhealthy food. This can be combined with regulations on how much sugar and salt can be added to food and drink and requirements for manufacturers to clearly show sugar and salt content and calories together with health warnings as with tobacco products.

The above includes all the necessary elements for answering this question with the identification of the problem as a market failure, the use of a diagram to explain it and the identification of two likely policies (responses) aimed at solving the problem.

However, there is always that bit extra that can be included in the quest to squeeze out an additional mark or two.

Possibilities here include:

- a fuller description of the negative consumption externalities associated with the consumption of unhealthy food;
- a fuller examination of the context in terms of the income group most likely to be affected (e.g. low-income groups).

There is a strong temptation here to consider differences between short-run and long-run effects as well as discussing the relative effectiveness of the policies *but* this needs to be resisted as such evaluation and discussion points must be left for part (b).

3 (b) Governments throughout the world are increasingly becoming concerned with the extent of negative consumption externalities which are responsible for a wide range of detrimental effects on society. The goods that generate these spill over costs to society are categorised as de-merit goods and the typical examples are the trio of tobacco, alcohol and drugs. More recently junk food and sugary drinks have been added to the list and a variety of policy measures have been implemented in many countries with the aim of reducing the level of consumption of these goods, such as those identified in part (a).

Any attempts by the government to influence consumption is viewed by some free market supporters and libertarian economists as undesirable leading to limitation of free choice and possibly less efficiency that is described as government failure.

In order to evaluate government policies which aim to influence consumption it is first necessary to establish what potential justification there is for it and why the policy might be considered to be necessary. The policy can then be judged according to how successfully it achieves the stated aim. Even if the policy does succeed in achieving its aim it is still necessary to consider other aspects and effects of the policy in both the short run and the long run. Policies often have undesirable effects on stakeholders that were not anticipated or accounted for in the initial decision.

For example, it has been estimated that when Mexico introduced a tax on sugary drinks in 2014 there was an initial decrease in consumption for two years but by 2017 consumption of these drinks had returned to the pre-tax levels. It is interesting to note that when the UK adopted a sugar tax policy in 2018 it was not apparently aiming at a direct impact on consumption but rather applying the principles embodied in nudge theory. By preannouncing the intended tax rates on added sugar according to the amount of added sugar the government succeeded in 'nudging' the manufacturers to reduce the sugar content of their drinks. The policy is considered to have been successful and it is estimated that over the next five years sugar content in soft drinks will be reduced by around 40%, leading to a reduction in obesity of half a million persons.

Unlike taxes on tobacco and alcohol, sugar taxes in the UK do not appear to be intended as a major source of tax revenue. Their aim is to incentivise producers to reformulate their products and to further achieve this aim, the UK government has been encouraged to introduce measures to compel manufacturers to clearly label sugar content and risks of obesity and diabetes in the same way that tobacco products have health warnings. The implication of this is that a combination of market-based policies and rules and regulations is likely to be more successful than just one or the other. In addition, the tax revenues can be used to finance an education and advertising program that promotes a healthier diet and lifestyle.

The fact that such a combination of policies can be effective in reducing the consumption of the de-merit goods does not however, guarantee the overall effectiveness of the policies. For a more appropriate evaluation a broader assessment needs to be made. Firstly, consideration needs to be given to how consumer spending will switch from the targeted products to other products. If reduced consumption of sugary drinks leads to increased consumption of beer or other alcoholic drinks, then there will be little if any benefit from the policy. Similarly, if reduced consumption of tobacco and alcohol leads to more use of addictive drugs or junk food and sugary drinks, little will have been gained. Simply transferring consumption from one set of de-merit goods to another set cannot be seen as an effective policy. The replacing of sugar by artificial sweeteners is also a controversial issue as some studies have shown that they can be addictive and can lead to consumers no longer enjoying healthy fresh fruit and vegetables. A study by the NHS in Britain indicated that consumers of products with artificial sweeteners experienced more weight gain than consumers of sugary drinks.

In the case of high taxes on tobacco and alcohol aimed at discouraging consumption there is evidence that high prices result in increased smuggling and illegal production. In Canada during the early 1990s taxes on cigarettes increased from $1.90 to $3.50 per pack and as a result there was a significant increase in smuggling of cigarettes so that approximately one third of all cigarette consumption was smuggled. It is estimated that over 50% of alcohol consumed in Sweden, which has very high alcohol tax, is from the illegal parallel market. This market also includes illicit production of high health risky alcohol using industrial alcohol and other dubious ingredients.

Apart from these problems there are also the effects on income distribution and family poverty to consider. Studies have shown that consumption of tobacco, alcohol, junk food and sugary drinks is predominantly by low income groups so that increased taxation of these products will have a marked regressive effect leading to equity concerns as income inequality will increase. Low income families may end up spending more on the higher taxed products which will leave less income available for other goods such as those related to education and health care. This could lead to a fall in living standards and an increase in child poverty.

Finally, there is the possible impact on manufacturers and retailers to consider. In the UK many of the de-merit goods such as cigarettes, sugary drinks and unhealthy snack food are sold in local corner shops which also provide milk and bread and other essential items. By limiting the demand for the profitable de-merit goods many of these shops will be forced to close down thus depriving the elderly and less mobile members of the local community with access to their daily shopping requirements. This is a major disadvantage for people who do not have a car and are unable to travel long distances to shop at supermarkets.

From the above it is clear that several factors need to be considered when evaluating the effectiveness of any policy as a variety of stakeholders will be affected in different ways and this makes it difficult to assess the net benefits or losses.

In the case of unhealthy food and sugary drinks it is possible that the government is viewing the problem incorrectly. The policy aim could possibly focus more on encouraging the consumption of healthy food and water rather than attempting to limit consumption of unhealthy food and drink. A more successful policy might be to subsidise healthy food and encourage the consumption of water as an alternative to sugary drinks.

This type of question can include a wide variety of relevant information and there is a limit to how much can reasonably be included in the time available. Additional evaluation points could be some analysis of price and income elasticity of demand in relation to taxation and the incidence on consumers. Additional diagrams could be included such as a subsidy diagram. Alternative effects on other stakeholders could also be identified and evaluated such as the tobacco industry and junk food industry workers who might lose their jobs as a result of the policy measures. Finally, to give a greater global perspective the effects on tobacco farmers and sugar farmers in LEDCs could also be included.

There is a significant amount of relevant information that can be presented and analysed for this type of question and you are not expected to include everything. The major difficulty that most students will face is the recollection of appropriate real-world examples that is a requirement of the question.

Question 4

(a) Explain two ways a government might respond to the existence of excessive monopoly power in a market. [10 marks]

(b) Using real-world examples discuss the extent to which markets which are dominated by large firms are undesirable. [15 marks]

This is a market failure question that would only appear on a Higher Level paper.

Answer

4 (a) A pure monopoly exists when there is only one firm in the industry which faces the entire market demand as its own and where there are effective barriers to prevent the entry of competing firms. However, for practical purposes any dominant firm in an industry which has a relatively large share of the market is able to exercise monopoly power. The existence of monopoly power is considered to be a type of market failure and there is therefore a potential justification for some form of government intervention aimed at correcting the market failure. As shown in diagram 1, a profit-maximising monopoly will produce a lower output with a higher price than if the market were perfectly competitive leading to a welfare loss represented by the area ABC.

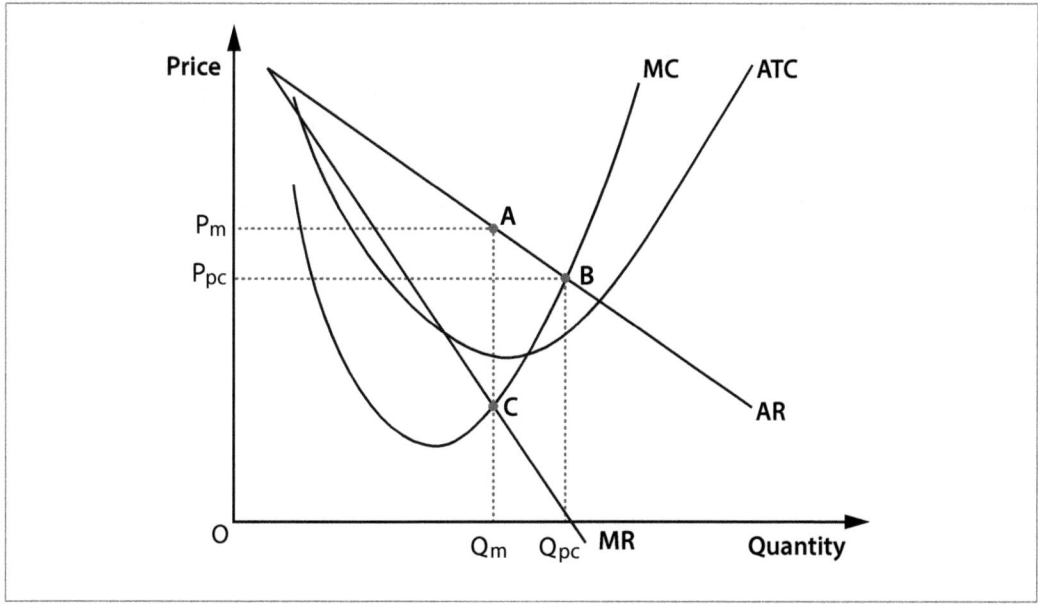

Diagram 1

In a perfectly competitive market the price would be equal to marginal cost at P_{pc} and the corresponding quantity would be at Q_{pc}. A profit-maximising monopolist however, would produce output Q_m where MC=MR and the corresponding price would be at P_m. This means that faced with the same costs a perfectly competitive industry will have a lower price and a higher output than a monopoly.

Many countries, including the USA and the EU have a range of policy measures aimed at preventing or reducing the potential exploitation of monopoly power. One policy is to prevent the development of monopoly power through legislation that does not permit firms having a sufficiently large share of the market so that they can influence the market at the expense of the consumer and competitors. These laws allow the authorities to investigate any firm which has more than 25% of the market and also to decide whether any proposed merger or takeover between firms will produce excessive monopoly power and limit competition. The European Commission is currently considering whether to allow a proposed merger between The Fiat Chrysler Automobile (FCA) group and the Peugeot SA (PSA) car manufacturer over concerns that it might restrict competition in the light commercial vehicle sector of the car market.

A second policy approach is to allow the existence of the monopoly power but to ensure that the power is not used to exploit the consumer and restrict competition. This can be achieved by limiting the firm's ability to set price. Theoretically, it could be possible to force the monopolist to set price equal to MC which would remove the welfare loss entirely and achieve allocative efficiency. In diagram 1 this would involve setting price at P_{pc} instead of at P_m. Alternatively the monopolist could be prevented from setting price at P_m and allowing only a given percentage mark-up above average cost.

The difficulty in formulating any appropriate policy is deciding what constitutes excessive monopoly power. Diagram 1 could be illustrating a firm in short-run equilibrium in monopolistic competition or a collusive oligopoly or a monopoly. There is no way of identifying what constitutes excessive monopoly power simply by looking at the diagram because according to diagram 1 it would be equally legitimate to restrict any firm that is not perfectly competitive.

4 (b) Although small firms such as shops are the most numerous in developed economies, the majority of output in terms of value is produced by large firms, many of which are dominant in the particular market in which they operate. The prevalence of large firms, especially in manufacturing, suggests that there are certain advantages related to size and market domination. The important question to consider is whether the advantages are confined to the firms or whether they are shared by consumers as well. In the UK and many other European countries, the food and household goods retailing industry is dominated by a few large supermarket chains. In the UK, the market is dominated by 4 companies of which Tesco is the largest with a market share of 20% in 2020 which is way ahead of Sainsbury's 15% in second place. These large-scale enterprises are able to earn significant economies of scale and as a result are able to offer a wide range of food products at lower prices than the smaller monopolistically competitive food retailers found in town centres and high streets. A similar situation exists in France where the top 5 supermarket chains share just under 80% of the market with Leclerc and Carrefour leading the field each with a 20% share of the market. The important question is whether this high degree of market domination in food retailing is in any way undesirable for consumers and the economy. There is no simple answer and it depends on several factors and the relative importance of the criteria that are applied for the evaluation.

Evaluation of market structures usually involves consideration of the following criteria: efficiency, price and output, choice and variety and dynamic innovation through research and development (R&D). In the case of food retailing a realistic evaluation would be to compare dominant supermarkets with grocery shops in monopolistically competitive markets, rather than a perfectly competitive market. With respect to allocative efficiency it is impossible to exist in any non-perfectly competitive profit-maximising firm. For any firm facing a downward sloping demand the profit-maximising price will always be above marginal cost so allocative efficiency cannot be achieved. If the alternative to dominant supermarkets was a perfectly competitive structure this allocative inefficiency would be important but since the alternative is a different form of imperfect competition it will also be allocatively inefficient. With respect to productive efficiency which is achieved when a firm produces at the minimum average cost where AC=MC it is necessarily true that this will never be achieved in long-run equilibrium in monopolistic competition because freedom of entry and exit means that firms can only earn normal profit with AR tangent to AC to the left of where MC=AC. With large scale dominant firms, it is quite likely that absolute cost levels will be lower and there is a possibility that firms may operate at a level of output that is closer to the minimum AC. These same considerations would apply to the car industry, shipbuilding, aircraft manufacturing, mining, petrol refining and a wide range of other industries with dominant firms. For example, breaking up Toyota or Boeing into many smaller monopolistically competitive firms would not improve efficiency as the average costs of these small firms would be much higher leading to higher prices which would also be above marginal costs.

In some industries such as rail transport and electricity supply to customers the cost advantage to one dominant producer is so great that they are described as natural monopolies. One way of ensuring that these natural monopolies do not exploit their power is to nationalise them so that they operate in the national interest rather than as profit maximisers. However, with the domination of neo-classical economic theories since the 1980s privatisation of state-run industries has been widely introduced as a supply side policy measure intended to increase efficiency. Since privatisation of the railways in the UK, accidents have increased and there is significant dissatisfaction among commuters regarding the quality and efficiency of the rail service. In many cases privatisation has led to a reduction in service quality and higher prices, for example with household gas in the UK.

With respect to price and output, the traditional comparison with perfect competition which assumes the same costs of production indicates that price will always be lower and output higher as clearly shown in diagram 1 in part (a). However, the same cost assumption is highly unrealistic and as already stated the alternative is monopolistic competition and not perfect competition. Large scale dominant firms will normally have much lower costs than small monopolistically competitive firms. Prices in supermarkets will generally be lower than prices in high street grocers and supermarkets are likely to have a much larger range of products than small food shops. Lower prices will increase consumer surplus and will normally be seen as advantageous for consumers, but sometimes this might not be case. In the UK the large supermarkets are able to exert considerable pressure on suppliers to cut their prices with the result that some suppliers are forced out of business. For example, dairy farmers have been forced to sell their milk at prices close to or even below cost so that supermarkets can sell cheap milk to customers. However, not all consumers see this as a benefit and some would be willing to pay higher prices in order to ensure fair prices for suppliers.

Finally, there is the factor of dynamic growth and innovation through R&D. it seems to be much more likely that large dominant firms will both have a greater ability and incentive to engage in R&D leading to new and improved products, compared to monopolistically or perfectly competitive firms which are unable to maintain supernormal profit in the long-run. There have clearly been much more significant innovations in industries characterised by large dominant firms such as pharmaceuticals, mobile telephony, computers, social media and car manufacturing than in typically more competitive markets such as hairdressing, fast food, and fruit and vegetable production. Monopoly power is much more likely to lead to dynamic economic growth through the process of 'creative destruction' identified by Schumpeter than perfectly or monopolistically competitive markets.

On balance, consumers are likely to benefit from the existence of large dominant firms in certain industries despite the potential dangers of exploitation of monopoly power. UK supermarkets have in the past engaged in price fixing of certain key products which acts against the consumer's interests. However, prices were still lower than in smaller food retailers and the fixed prices ultimately encouraged the entry of lower cost foreign competitors such as Lidl and Aldi which forced all supermarkets to lower prices.

Both Google and Facebook are dominant firms with a high degree of monopoly power but consumers are not exploited by high prices as a result, in fact they face zero prices and are provided with an efficient and desirable service. If there were hundreds of alternative search engines and hundreds of alternative social media platforms, would consumers be better served? Overall, the gains from large dominant firms are likely to outweigh the potential losses as a result of the abuse of monopoly power.

This is a rather difficult question that although already quite long could be even longer, as there are additional points and diagrams that could be used to supplement the analysis. For example: a diagram showing long-run equilibrium in monopolistic competition, a diagram showing a natural monopoly, a diagram showing economies of scale and/or a diagram showing the effect on price and output with a significant cost reduction when a competitive industry becomes a monopoly as shown below.

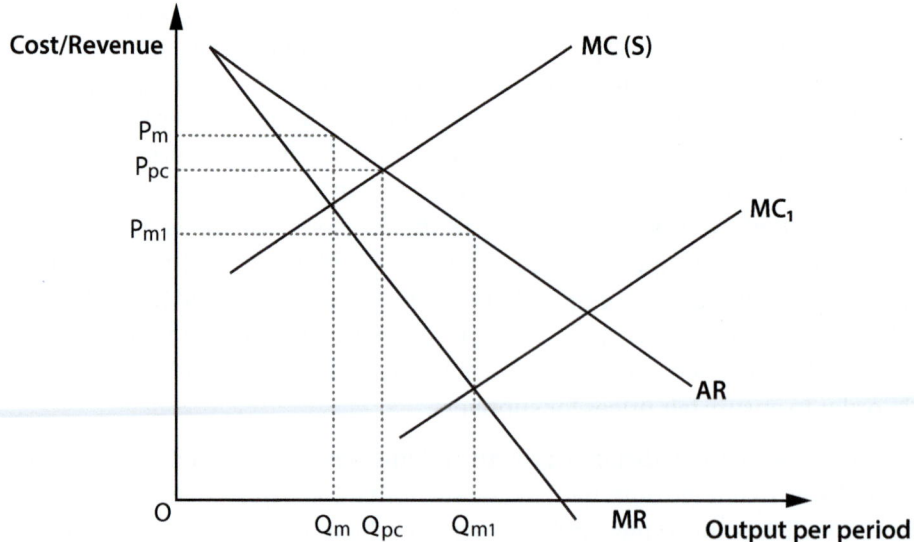

This is a very useful diagram to learn as it can be used to compare all market structures with respect to price and output depending on whether costs remain the same or whether they fall. If a competitive industry becomes a monopoly or a collusive oligopoly and as a result there is a significant reduction in costs from MC to MC_1 then price will be lower at PM_1 and output higher at QM_1 than the competitive combination P_{pc} and Q_{pc}. If comparing perfect competition and monopolistic competition you would restrict the analysis to MC as there is no greater scope for economies of scale in monopolistic competition. If comparing monopolistic competition with monopoly then P_m and Q_m would reflect price and output in monopolistic competition while P_{m1} and Q_{m1} would apply to a monopoly (or any dominant firm in an oligopoly).

Finally, the conclusion will depend to a large extent on the real-world examples that are used. Most of my examples support that large dominant firms are likely to be more desirable than smaller firms, but this might not be the case in all industries and there are potential advantages associated with small firms such as quality of service and convenience. However, you are not expected to know or include such a large number of examples and the aim is to strike a balance between the predictions of economic theory and real-world situations. Economic theory suggests that allocative efficiency is of great significance but a question that I frequently ask my classes is 'When was the last time you were in a shop and asked whether the price of a product was equal to MC?' followed by 'Who would rather pay P_{pc} which is equal to MC than P_{m1} which is above MC with respect to the diagram above?' As mentioned in part (a) since the practical alternative to monopoly or a dominant firm in oligopoly is monopolistic competition, allocative efficiency ceases to be an issue of any significance.

The current economic recession that is beginning to impact the world economy as a result of the Covid-19 pandemic has shown that large firms are much more able to survive than small firms, many of which have already closed down.

2.2 Unit 3 Macroeconomics

Question 5

(a) Explain two possible causes of inflation. [10 marks]

(b) Using real-world examples, evaluate the effectiveness of demand side policies to achieve low inflation. [15 marks]

This is a typical macro question that could appear on either the HL or SL paper.

Answer

5(a) Inflation is defined as a persistent or continuous increase in the average price level over time and is expressed as a percentage change derived from a weighted consumer price index (CPI) that seeks to measure changes in the cost of living. The average price level is determined by the interaction of aggregate demand (AD) and aggregate supply (AS) and there are therefore two potential causes of inflation. One is a shift in AD to the right, known as demand-pull inflation and the other is a shift in AS to the left known as cost-push inflation.

Demand-pull inflation can be caused by any increase in a component of AD such as consumption or Investment or government spending or exports. For example, an increase in consumer confidence would stimulate an increase in consumer spending which other things being equal would cause AD to shift to the right as shown in diagram 1.

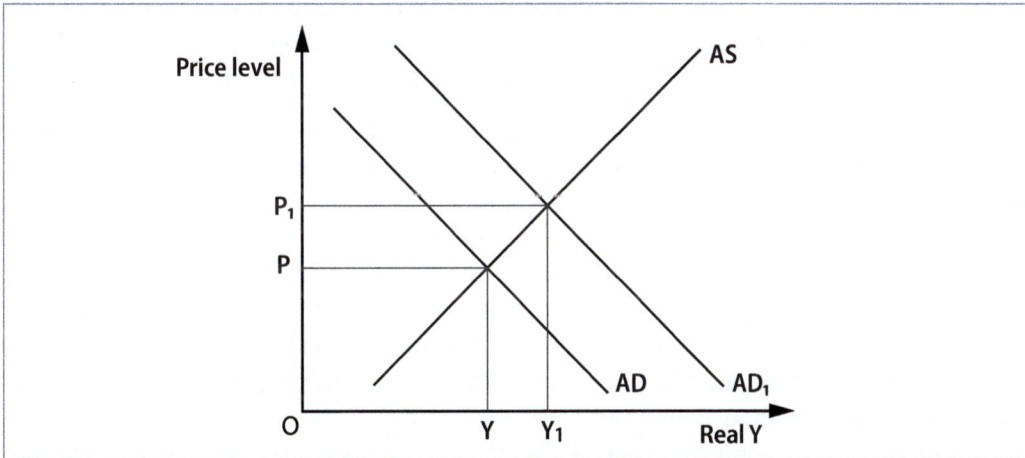

Diagram 1

Any increase in one or more of these components will shift AD to the right to AD_1 and as a result the price level rises from P to P_1. At the same time real income also rises to Y_1. Rising demand has the effect of pulling prices up and the extent of the price increase will be determined by the slope of AS. The steeper the AS, the greater the price increase.

The second major type of inflation occurs when costs of production in the economy are rising thus causing firms to cut back their output. This is represented by the shift in AS to the left in diagram 2.

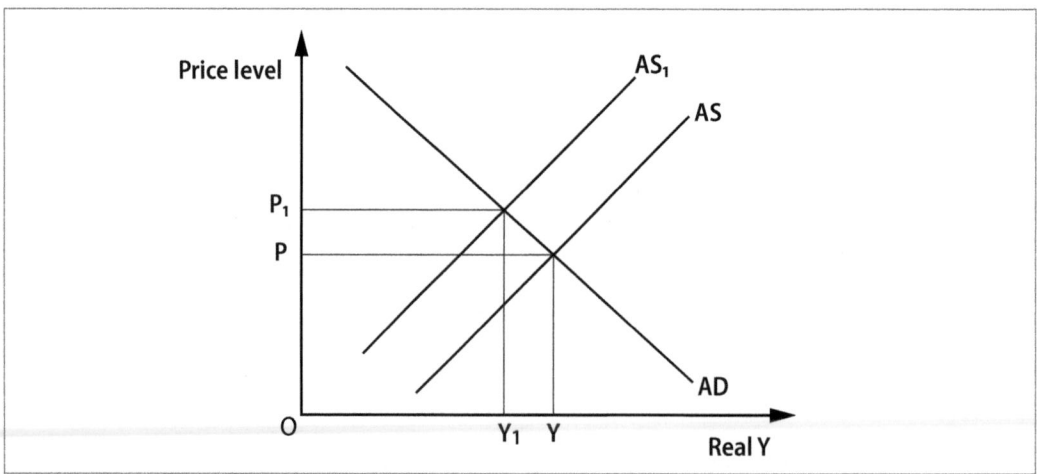

Diagram 2

The shift in AS to AS₁ causes prices to rise from P to P₁ thus creating inflationary pressure, while at the same time real income falls to Y₁. Costs of production can increase as a result of rising costs of imported oil or raw materials, increases in wages above productivity or even an increase in expenditure taxes such as VAT. The extent of cost-push inflation will depend on the magnitude of the cost increase together with the slope of AD and the extent to which it leads to further inflationary pressure as workers demand compensatory increases in wages. Cost-push inflation is the result of the short-run AS shifting to the left which requires that the increase in production costs is something that will affect many firms in the economy. For example, an increase in the price of milk would increase costs of production for cheese and yoghurt producers but would not be significant enough to cause the SRAS to shift. In contrast an increase in oil prices would affect transport costs that would have an impact on the whole economy and cause SRAS to shift.

5 (b) Ever since the experience of rising unemployment and inflation, known as stagflation, in the 1970s, two important changes in macroeconomic policy initiatives have occurred. The first was the prioritising of control of inflation over unemployment and the second was the gradual rejection of fiscal policy with greater emphasis being placed on monetary policy and subsequently supply-side policies. These changes are closely linked to the rise of monetarism, popularised by M. Friedman, which also inspired the adoption of neo-classical non-interventionist policy recommendations. During the 1980s both the UK and the USA authorities implemented monetary and supply-side policies aimed at achieving low inflation combined with economic growth. Since 2000, this objective appears to have been achieved since neither the US nor the UK has experienced inflation above 4% and for most years' inflation has been below the 2% target. Control of inflation is still a major objective of government policy despite the fact that since the global recession of 2008 deflation rather than inflation has been more of a threat.

Like many countries the UK has an inflation target of 2% which the Central Bank is responsible for achieving. It does this through its implementation of monetary policy which involves changes in the rate of interest in order to influence spending in the economy. If there is pressure for inflation to rise above the 2% target the Central Bank will manipulate the money supply in order to cause the rate of interest to rise. This can be achieved by intervention in the money market through sales of Treasury bills or Bonds that will limit the liquidity available to commercial banks and force them to cut back on credit creation and so reducing the money supply leading to an increase in interest rates. Such a policy is known as open market operations and monetary policy is a major demand-side policy measure that is used for the control of inflation. Another type of demand-side policy is fiscal policy which involves changes in government spending relative to taxation with the aim of influencing the level of AD. Such policies are specifically targeted at relieving demand pull pressures and aim to have a deflationary or contractionary effect on AD. By reducing the level of government spending relative to taxation there will be a direct effect on AD as shown in diagram 3. In contrast, monetary policy through the increase in interest rates does not have a direct effect on AD. It will only cause AD to fall if it causes a reduction in consumer spending or some other component of AD. Consumption is thought to be interest sensitive because a certain proportion of spending is financed by credit such as loans to buy houses or consumer durables like cars. The higher the rate of interest charged for these loans, the lower the demand for them so by raising interest rates, the Central Bank hopes to shift AD to the left. A similar result can be achieved by a contractionary fiscal policy which involves reducing the level of Government spending relative to Taxation. The effects are shown in diagram 3.

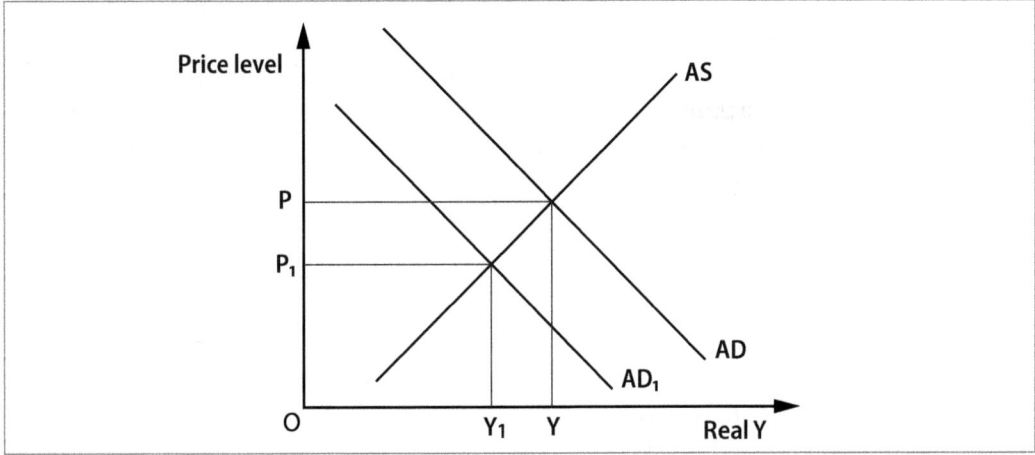

Diagram 3

By shifting AD to the left to AD_1, inflationary pressure is reduced as the price level falls to P_1, but at the same time the level of output and real income in the economy falls to Y_1. This means that unemployment will increase, and this is a definite disadvantage of deflationary demand management. In addition, increasing interest rates might have some further negative effects. Investment spending by firms is also inversely related to interest rates and so any increase in interest rates will reduce Investment and this will further reduce AD. Since investment constitutes spending on capital, which is a factor of production, the reduction in investment will cause the long-run AS to shift to the left as well and this is clearly an undesirable consequence of such a policy.

Higher interest rates will also attract an inflow of short-term financial capital, known as 'hot' money and this will cause the exchange rate of the currency to appreciate. As a result, exports will become more expensive and less competitive while imports will become cheaper and more competitive. Depending on the price elasticity of demand for exports and imports, this could lead to a current account deficit together with a loss of output and employment in the export industries. One potential advantage however, for a country that imports oil and raw materials, is that the lower import prices will reduce production costs, and this could stimulate the supply side of the economy. Through the effect of higher interest rates on the exchange rate, a contractionary monetary policy can thus be effective in controlling both demand-pull and cost-push inflation. In contrast, a contractionary fiscal policy will at best be able to reduce demand-pull inflation only.

Monetary policy has other advantages compared to fiscal policy for example it is much more flexible and easier to change in desired incremental adjustments. It works relatively quickly and does not have a negative effect on the budget deficit, which is a major constraint on fiscal policy. However, both fiscal and monetary policies, if successful in controlling inflation, will exert a recessionary effect on growth and employment leading to conflicts between policy objectives. This is clearly shown in diagram 3 with the shift in AD leading to a fall in real income from Y to Y_1. Monetary policy has the further disadvantage of influencing the exchange rate which can create further policy objective conflicts through its effect on the current account balance and the export sector.

Another aspect of monetary policy that is relevant to its long-term effectiveness is the effect it has on perceptions and expectations. Central banks like to be pro-active and will seek to adjust interest rates in anticipation of future inflation rather than as a response to actual inflation which has risen above the target level. This approach can lead to conflicts with other government policy objectives as occurred in 2018 in the USA when the Federal Reserve raised interest rates in four stages from 1.75% in March to 2.5% in December. These increases were strongly criticised by President Trump who was concerned that it would interfere with his growth stimulus policy as well as his trade policy because it caused the strengthening of the dollar which undermined his plan to stimulate US exports and reduce imports in order to reduce the current account deficit. This tight monetary policy was intended to prevent the economy from overheating leading to inflation, and it did coincide with a slowdown in growth so that during 2019 the policy was reversed. Subsequently, with the huge disruption of the Corona-virus pandemic on the global economy the Federal Reserve along with other Central Banks throughout the world have slashed interest rates to a minimum.

Overall, the effectiveness of demand-side policies in achieving low inflation will depend on a variety of factors. They will be more effective if the inflation is predominantly demand-pull and less so if the inflation is imported cost-push. Of the two alternatives monetary policy is considered to be more appropriate and potentially more effective for reasons of flexibility and quicker response time. However, both policies have serious limitations with respect to conflicts with other policy objectives such as growth and full employment. Monetary policy might also conflict with trade objectives through the impact of interest rates on the exchange rate and if the inflation is caused by high levels of consumer spending inspired by optimistic confidence, it is unlikely that realistically modest increases in interest rates will be very effective in deterring this spending.

Although a rather straight-forward type of evaluation question it is made difficult by the need to find relevant and appropriate real-world examples. This is especially difficult since no major economy has had to control high inflation in recent years and in fact the opposite has been the main experience with Japan and certain EU countries experiencing deflation since the financial crisis of 2008. This means that the most relevant examples of monetary policy are for expansionary stimulus programs through methods such as quantitative easing. An alternative approach might be to refer to the two fairly recent examples of hyper-inflation in Zimbabwe and Venezuela, but these are examples of how excessive increases in the money supply (printing money) can cause inflation rather than how inflation can be cured.

The actual workings of monetary policy can be quite complex and for the current new syllabus students are expected to have a fairly detailed knowledge of money market equilibrium conditions and tools such as open market operations and quantitative easing. However, the essence and importance of monetary policy is through the adjustment of interest rates and this is the key concept that needs to be analysed.

An important point to note is also that although presented as a government policy, monetary policy is in most countries independent of the government and is implemented by the Central Bank which is responsible for achieving the inflation target. This independence is an important feature of the policy but the principle has been severely tested in the USA recently under president Trump who has repeatedly criticised the Federal Reserve and has tried to influence its policy recommendations to suit his political agenda.

A final point to note is the role of expectations and perceptions in the formulation of monetary policy. For days before the Central Bank meets to review its monetary policy stance there will be speculation about what the likely decision will be taking into account current and predicted economic data. If it is expected that interest rates will be increased at the next meeting speculators will begin buying the currency in anticipation of this event and as a result the exchange rate will increase days before the interest rate decision is even made. Similarly, the Central Bank might set its monetary policy with the aim of influencing expectations and perceptions. For example, by increasing interest rates by 25 points (0.25%) even when inflation is below the 2% target rate, the Bank might be trying to send a message that the economy has strong growth potential with the aim of inspiring confidence. In this way the policy might be used to 'nudge' consumer and business confidence towards optimism, although it is a dangerous policy that could backfire.

Question 6

(a) Explain the causes and nature of cyclical and structural unemployment. [10 marks]

(b) Using real-world examples, evaluate the effectiveness of fiscal policy to achieve low unemployment. [15 marks]

Again, this is a typical question that could be set on either the HL or SL paper.

Answer

6(a) Unemployment is measured as the percentage of the working population that is able and willing to work, but is unable to find a job. Economists identify two categories of unemployment: equilibrium and disequilibrium. Frictional, structural and seasonal are the three types of unemployment in the first category which collectively makes up what is referred to as the natural rate of unemployment (the amount of unemployment that exists when the labour market is in equilibrium). Of these, structural unemployment is the most important and potentially problematic. There is only one type of disequilibrium unemployment which is cyclical or demand deficient.

Structural unemployment is caused by some structural change in the demand for a particular skill or type of labour in the economy. This could be the result of replacement of labour by capital because of some technological innovation. For example, production line workers being replaced by robots in car manufacturing or travel agencies being made redundant by online booking services. Alternatively, the change in demand could be the result of cheap imports that replace domestically produced goods. For example, during the 1990s the textile industry in many southern European countries faced intense competition from cheaper textiles from Asia and as firms closed down textile workers became structurally unemployed. This type of unemployment will persist unless labour is perfectly mobile, but there will usually be a mismatch between the available jobs in the economy and the available workers. The structurally unemployed might not have the skills needed for the available jobs or might be in a different geographical location than where the available jobs are. If workers are geographically and occupationally immobile then structural unemployment will persist.

Cyclical unemployment is associated with a recessionary gap which can develop in an economy when the level of aggregate demand (AD) is insufficient to purchase the full employment output of the economy. The equilibrium level of income (Y_e) is less than the full employment level of income (Y_f). This situation is shown in diagram 1.

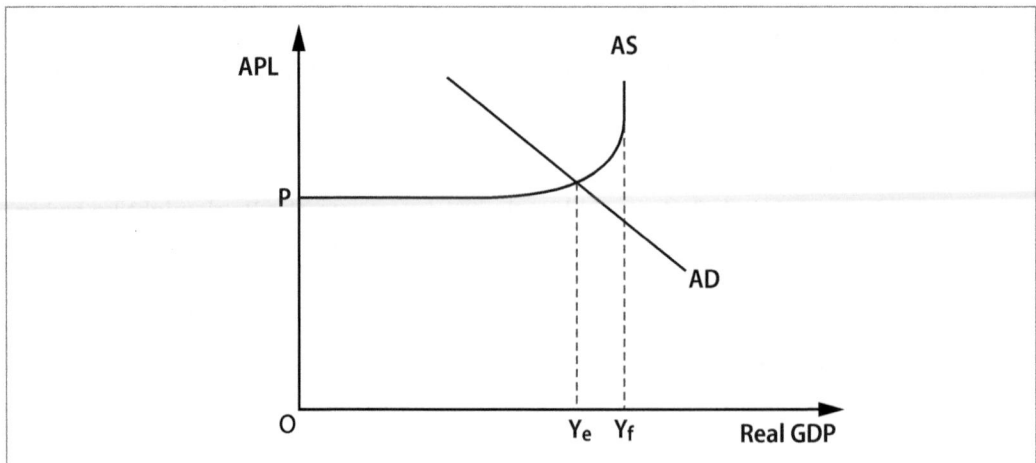

Diagram 1

The situation shown in diagram 1 with $Y_e < Y_f$ is equivalent to an economy operating within its production possibility boundary. Even if labour was perfectly mobile there are simply not enough available jobs for the available workers. If there were 1.5 million people unemployed in an economy and 600,000 job vacancies it would be possible to broadly identify 900,000 as cyclically unemployed and 600,000 as structurally unemployed.

6(b) Fiscal policy is a demand-side policy that aims to influence the level of AD through changes in the level of government spending and taxation. It therefore involves changes in the government's budget and has two components. One is automatic and the other is discretionary. If a country is entering the recessionary phase of the trade cycle characterised by falling demand and rising unemployment there will be an automatic corrective fiscal stimulus as a result of the structure of government spending and taxation. The extent of this automatic fiscal stimulus will vary from country to country. In Scandinavian countries that have relatively high levels of unemployment benefits and welfare payments combined with steeply progressive income taxes, falling incomes and rising unemployment will lead to a relatively large automatic increase in government spending coupled with a relatively large fall in tax revenues. Free market/ neoclassical economists consider such automatic stimuli to be sufficient and advocate no further fiscal action, but Keynesian economists would normally recommend additional discretionary fiscal measures which would involve specific increases in government spending and/or cuts in taxation. Inevitably, any such discretionary fiscal stimulus policy will lead to an increase in the budget deficit as the level of government spending will increase relative to tax revenues and this will increase the debt burden faced by future generations and if unchecked could become unsustainable. It is partly for this reason that neoclassical economists discourage the use of discretionary fiscal policy to achieve low unemployment and prefer to rely on monetary policy as a better short-term solution and supply-side policies for a more long-term solution.

In addition to the accumulated debt problem, neoclassical criticism of fiscal policy identifies the so called 'crowding out effect'. It is claimed that because an expansionary fiscal policy necessitates borrowing, the additional borrowing will cause the rate of interest to increase which in turn will lead to a decrease in consumption (C) and investment (I) spending. The increase in AD as a result of the fiscal stimulus will therefore be neutralised by the corresponding decrease in C and I. Real-world examples do not however seem to support the existence of such a crowding out effect. Since the global recession of 2008, most major economies in the world turned to fiscal policy in an attempt to boost demand and as a result the USA, Japan, the UK and several EU countries faced significant increases in their budget deficits. According to the crowding out theory the borrowing required to finance these historically high deficits should have led to significant increases in interest rates. In actual fact interest rates in all these deficit countries were at their historically lowest levels at around 0.5% or less. This apparent disparity between theory and practice can presumably be explained by the fact that if, as would normally be the case, an expansionary monetary policy was implemented together with the fiscal stimulus, interest rates would not increase and there would be no crowding out effect. This is in fact what most countries did in response to the recession following the financial crisis of 2008. Interest rates were lowered to near zero and when this was not sufficient to stimulate demand given low consumer and business confidence, the policy of quantitative easing (QE) was introduced in an attempt to encourage bank lending by increasing liquidity in the money market.

A similar policy is currently (July 2020) under way in the face of the recession caused by the Corona-virus pandemic. Central banks have responded with a renewed round of QE, but given the relative ineffectiveness of monetary policy in such situations, the main policy initiative is via a large fiscal stimulus which despite creating large budget deficits, has not led to an increase in interest rates and crowding out. How effective this fiscal stimulus will be in reducing unemployment is difficult to judge as the effects of the pandemic are ongoing, but it is probably the case that unemployment, which in many countries has currently risen above 10%, would be even higher without the fiscal policy initiatives that have been introduced. Even Germany, which has been a major opponent of fiscal deficits and has usually maintained a budget surplus, is expected to record a budget deficit of 7% this year with a fiscal stimulus package of around 1trillion euros, financed with a bond issue.

In less extreme circumstances, with a mild recession and unemployment at more manageable levels, the effectiveness of fiscal policy will depend on the type of unemployment that the country is facing. At best fiscal policy, by increasing AD will increase the demand for workers by creating more job vacancies. It could therefore be potentially effective in reducing demand deficient or cyclical unemployment. However, if the unemployment is mainly structural, simply increasing the number of available jobs will not be effective. To reduce this type of unemployment it is necessary to increase labour mobility and labour market flexibility, which can only be achieved with the successful implementation of supply-side policies. Since both fiscal policy and supply-side policies are relatively slow to have an effect, neither offer an effective short-term solution and at best will only be effective in the long run. Monetary policy works much more quickly and is more flexible than fiscal policy, but as noted ceases to be effective when interest rates are close to zero and consumer and business confidence is low.

Finally, a general problem faced by all policies is the potential conflict between policy objectives. Expansionary demand-side policies will conflict with the objective of price stability and current account balance, while supply-side policies will tend to conflict with the objective of greater income equality. No policy is without an opportunity cost but fiscal policy possibly has more limitations than the other alternatives. It has a long time lag, it leads to a future debt problem, it can be inflationary and if it successfully increases AD and income will lead to a deterioration of the current account balance as spending on imports will increase. Neoclassical economists would also claim that it causes crowding-out and since they assume that wages and prices are fully flexible in both directions, the economy will correct a recessionary gap with no need for a fiscal intervention. This neoclassical view may be rather optimistic, especially in extreme situations such as the deep recession following the 2008 financial crisis and the current recession with the pandemic. Even the most free market, conservative anti-Keynesian governments have openly embraced large fiscal stimulus packages to combat the deflationary effects of the demand shocks generated by these real-world situations which indicates that for all its failings, fiscal policy is the most effective policy to tackle extreme recessions.

Unlike the previous question there are very many recent examples of the use of fiscal policy to combat large recessionary gaps and it should be quite easy to find detailed examples to apply. At the time of writing, the full effects of the Corona-virus pandemic are still unknown, and it seems likely that countries will continue to use fiscal stimulus packages in an attempt to minimise the deflationary effects. Latest estimates are that the EU economies will shrink by more than 10% this year and experience levels of unemployment not seen since the Great Depression of the 1930s.

There are various diagrams that could be used to illustrate the analysis. An obvious example is a simple AD/AS diagram showing how an expansionary fiscal policy would shift AD to the right thus moving Y_e closer to Y_f and reducing the size of the recessionary gap. Students who want to show the possibility of a 'crowding-out' effect could show this with the above mentioned diagram together with a second AD shift to the left. It is also possible to use a labour market supply and demand diagram showing the disparity between the supply of labour and the labour force at the equilibrium wage rate in order to illustrate structural unemployment. However, in my experience very few students are actually taught this diagram.

Other alternatives include a neoclassical AD/AS model to show the self-correcting mechanism assumed to operate if wages and prices are fully flexible. Finally, a lot more detail could be included and the multiplier is also worthy of a mention as it amplifies the effect of any fiscal stimulus, but there is a limit to how much the average student can write and you are not expected to include every relevant point. The key as always is to provide a balanced discussion of the effectiveness of the policy with reference to appropriate real-world examples.

Question 7

(a) Explain two ways in which a higher rate of economic growth can be achieved. [10 marks]

(b) Using real-world examples evaluate the view that increased economic growth is desirable. [15 marks]

A typical growth question that could appear on either HL or SL exam papers.

Answer

7 (a) Economic growth refers to the rate of change in real GDP over time measured as a % change. Any increase in real GDP constitutes positive growth, but economists usually distinguish between two types of growth, actual and potential. Actual growth refers to any increase in real GDP over time and is associated with an increase in GDP as the economy

moves towards the full employment level of income (Y_f). It is equivalent to an economy moving from a point within its production possibility boundary towards the boundary. In contrast, potential growth refers to long-term growth represented by an outward shift of the boundary. This is equivalent to a rightward shift of the vertical long-run aggregate supply (LRAS).

Actual growth can be achieved by any increase in aggregate demand (AD) that moves the economy closer to Y_f. This could be the result of an increase in any component of AD. For example, an increase in consumer confidence would cause consumption spending to increase and AD would shift to AD_1 as shown in diagram 1.

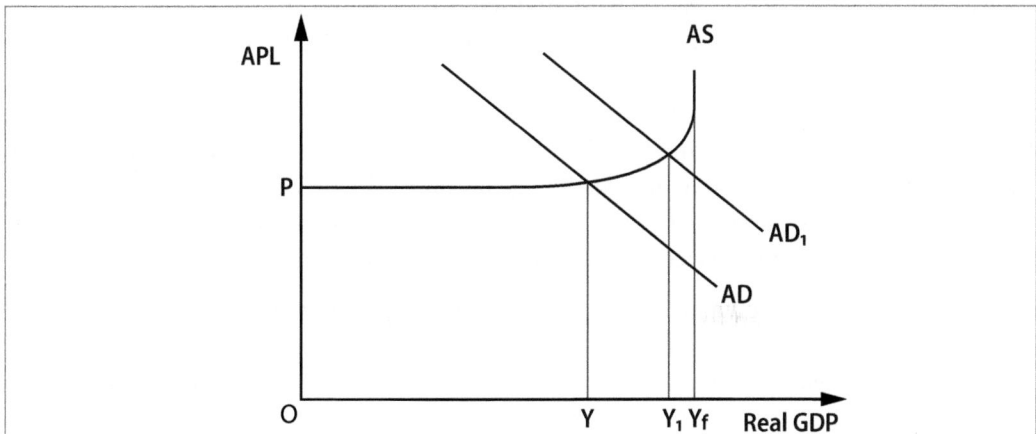

Diagram 1

The increase in AD to AD_1 leads to an increase in real GDP from Y to Y_1 which represents actual growth.

However, this type of growth has no impact on the productive potential of the economy which is determined by the position of the LRAS. Potential growth can only be achieved by an increase in the LRAS which in turn requires an increase in ether the quantity or the quality of the factors of production. For example, an increase in the training of workers will increase the efficiency of labour and this will shift LRAS to the right thus increasing the productive potential of the economy. The effect of this is shown in diagram 2.

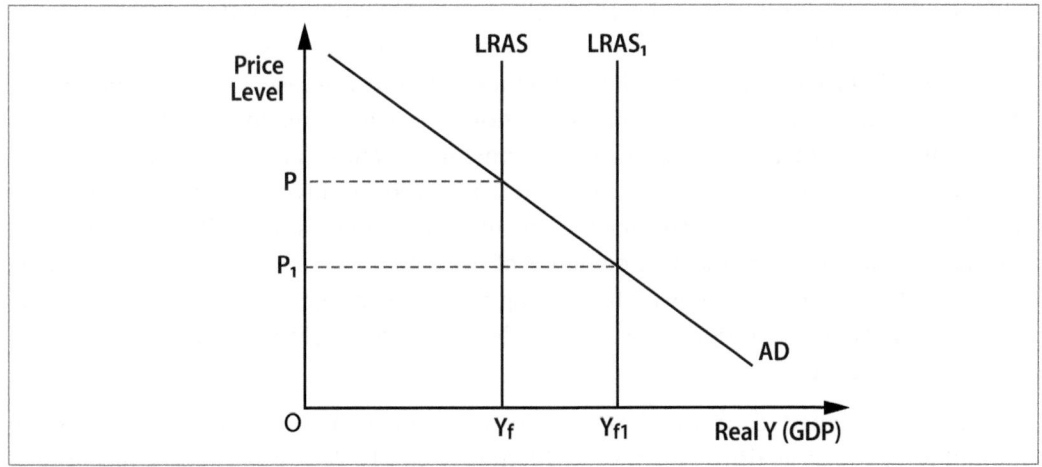

Diagram 2

By increasing the quality or efficiency of labour, the productive potential of the economy will be increased as shown by the shift in LRAS to $LRAS_1$. As a result the full employment level of income increases from Y_f to Y_{f1}.

Interestingly, an increase in investment by firms to create more capital will have the effect of generating both actual growth since investment is a component of AD, and potential growth since more capital will shift LRAS to the right as well.

The two ways that a higher rate of economic growth can be achieved are therefore either an increase in AD when equilibrium income is at less than full employment, or an increase in LRAS.

7 (b) Economic growth has traditionally been an important objective of government policy as it is taken to reflect a country's economic performance and efficiency while leading to increased income, output and employment together with a corresponding increase in the standard of living for the population. Potential growth is what brings the more permanent improvements in economic welfare and it is undeniable that sustained growth has contributed to significant advances in the quality of life and living standards in developed and developing countries. Countries that have experienced rapid growth recently include China, India and Brazil and in all these there has been a marked reduction in poverty and improvement in average living standards. In already developed countries, like the USA and EU, past growth has contributed to very high living standards with new and improved goods and services, increased life expectancy and better education.

This view however, is increasingly being questioned, especially in developed economies where the majority of people already enjoy a relatively high standard of living and where basic needs are easily satisfied. Once a country has achieved its basic requirements of universal well-being with no absolute poverty and high levels of health care and education, is it still necessary to pursue even further growth? The answer to this question requires a consideration of the opportunity cost of growth within the context of sustainability.

Growth is only worthwhile if it is sustainable. This means that it does not use up non-renewable resources and does not impose permanent damage on the environment and reduce the well-being of future generations.

The current problem of global warming and climate change is a result of uncontrolled growth, and there is much evidence to suggest that growth in China is adding a huge burden to the environment and leading to excessive, health threatening pollution. In China there are now many more car owners compared to 30 years ago and this is the result of high growth rates which have led to greatly increased incomes. 30 years ago, Chinese urban centres were full of people riding bicycles going to work and back. Nowadays, city centres are full of cars and motorised vehicles moving very slowly and creating dangerously high levels of atmospheric pollution. Is the Chinese car owner better off than the bicycle owner of the previous generation? Has car ownership actually improved the quality of life of the average Chinese consumer? These are important questions which are not easy to answer and are in the realm of normative economics which rely on value judgements. The recent lockdowns in many cities as a result of the Corona-virus pandemic has provided clear evidence of the extent of atmospheric pollution. The absence of traffic on roads allowed for a smog free atmosphere with pictures appearing in the media of clear skies that were now visible in normally polluted places such as New Delhi and Shanghai.

Growth in developed countries has also fostered the expansion of consumption of harmful goods such as drugs, alcohol and fattening foods. As a result, some developed countries are experiencing a decline in life expectancy. In addition, there is the important question of who actually benefits from growth. There is strong evidence that since the 1980s income inequality in the USA and the UK has increased which is to some extent linked to the growth promoting supply-side policies that were adopted. If growth is not shared equally within and between countries, it can lead to resentment and social conflict. Governments need to look at the distribution of income and wealth and not just its creation.

For LDCs, growth is necessary for development but it must not be at the expense of quality of life and sustainability. For developed countries, there is no great urgency for unregulated growth. More consideration needs to be given to quality of life and, therefore, a balance of objectives is advisable. Unemployment and inflation are serious problems and should not be sacrificed for growth.

Growth needs to be shared more evenly within and between countries and should not be pursued at the expense of policies which genuinely improve the quality of life of the average person. It should not be given top priority as a policy objective.

This does not mean that growth is not desirable, but that it needs to be assessed within a wider context that includes important factors such as sustainability, equity, quality of life and well-being. Growth is only desirable if it improves the lives of the majority meaningfully and sustainably, it should be seen as a means to an end and not as an end in itself as was the case in the past.

Global warming and climate change are closely linked to growth as are contributary factors such as deforestation. In Brazil the destruction of the Amazon rain forests has contributed to the growth of the economy as agricultural production has increased on the de-forested areas, but this is having a major negative impact on the global environment. Many academics and experts think that the Covid-virus pandemic is indirectly linked to the drive for growth through intensive farming and animal food production. As a result there is increasing support for a return to smaller scale environmentally friendly methods of production instead of large scale intensive methods which are more growth oriented. Economists have been pointing out the potential costs of economic growth for many years and as early as 1967 the Stanford economist E.J. Mishan explored this in his ground-breaking book *The Costs of Economic Growth*. It is only more recently however, that these costs have begun to be taken more seriously with the ever more frequent extreme climatic conditions and disasters, coupled with the melting of the ice cap and mountain glaciers.

Controlled, sustainable and regulated economic growth may still be desirable but the social and environmental costs need to be effectively measured in comparison to the benefits.

This is now a very well documented topic and there should be no serious problem in finding appropriate real-world examples to support your analysis in part (b).

For part (a) and for any question relating to growth it is always advisable to make the distinction between actual and potential growth. Actual growth can be seen as short-term while potential growth is long-term. This distinction makes it easier to relate growth to government policy as questions will frequently ask you to evaluate which policies are more effective in achieving growth. As shown in my answer to part (a) actual growth can be achieved with any expansionary demand side policy that shifts AD to the right. Long-term or potential growth, however, can only be achieved by shifting the LRAS which requires a successful supply-side policy.

As with all questions, an alternative approach can be taken and climate change deniers or supporters of Trump and Bolsonaro could argue that growth is always desirable and that the costs are exaggerated. It might be more difficult to come up with effective real-world examples however, to support this viewpoint and remember that the typical IB examiner is not likely to accept 'fake' examples or to be impressed with unsupported dogmatic opinions.

Question 8

(a) Explain two ways that a more equal distribution of income and wealth can be achieved. [10 marks]

(b) Using real-world examples evaluate the view that policies aimed at reducing inequality will always be at the expense of economic efficiency and growth. [15 marks]

Answer

8 (a) Achieving a more equal distribution of income is sometimes a stated objective of government policy although in reality very little is done to achieve it. In both the UK and the USA there has been a documented increase in income inequality since the 1980s which is possibly linked to the implementation of supply side policies and in particular changes in taxation policy. Wealth and income are closely related but wealth inequalities tend to be even greater than income inequalities because wealth is usually inherited in the form of fixed assets such as property or financial assets such as investment portfolios.

One way of making the distribution of income more equal would be to make the system of taxation more progressive so that a larger proportion of income is paid by those who have higher incomes. This requires an increase in the average tax rate which can best be achieved by increasing the marginal tax rates on income tax while at the same time reducing indirect taxation relative to direct taxation. Indirect taxes are regressive because the amount of tax paid when an item is purchased is the same for everyone and is unrelated to income whereas direct taxes like income tax can be levied at a higher rate on higher incomes.

Shifting the balance of taxation towards direct from indirect taxes would reduce income inequalities which would be reflected in a decrease in the numerical value of the Gini coefficient and a corresponding shift in the Lorenz curve towards the line of perfect equality from A to B as shown in diagram 1.

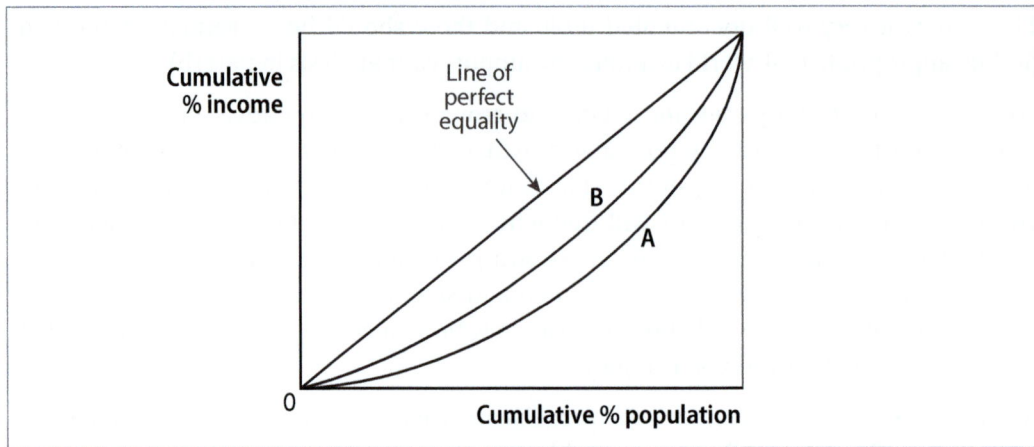

Diagram 1

Perfect equality would be achieved if the Lorenz curve was on the line of perfect equality in which case the Gini coefficient would be equal to zero so the smaller the number the more equal the distribution of income. The UK has a Gini coefficient of 0.33 (2017) up from 0.28 in 1979, while the USA has a figure of 0.41 (2016) up from 0.34 in 1979.

Since a large proportion of a household's wealth is inherited, an effective way of increasing the equality of wealth would be with an inheritance tax which then distributed the revenues to low income households in the form of transfer payments such as unemployment benefits or income supplements.

By changing the balance of taxation towards direct progressive taxes and introducing or increasing the taxation of inherited wealth and spending the revenue on benefits to low income households it is possible to increase the equality of both income and wealth distribution, but as will be analysed in part (b) there are certain objections to the implementation of such policies.

8(b) Economic efficiency is very important for the performance of an economy and its ability to achieve steady and sustainable growth. Many economists and in particular those who support the neoclassical school of thought are concerned that policies such as those identified in part (a) will have the effect of reducing the level of economic efficiency and limit the rate of growth. Neoclassical economists generally support supply-side policies aimed at making markets operate more freely and with a higher degree of flexibility, especially for labour markets. Such policies include reducing or removing minimum wages and unemployment benefits with the aim of increasing the incentive for unemployed workers to find jobs while increasing the number of available jobs. This would give a boost to the supply-side of the economy which would lead to an increase in long-run (potential) economic growth. Additional labour market supply-side policies include reducing the power of trade unions and increasing the use of part time rather than full time workers. These policies were introduced during the 1980s in the UK together with other supply-side policies such as decreasing progressive income taxes and increasing the balance of taxation towards indirect taxes. The increase in income inequality since then, as measured by the increase in the Gini coefficient, is closely linked to these policies which were aimed at promoting greater efficiency and growth.

Supply-side policies of this type can be seen to be in conflict with the objective of greater equality in the distribution of income and wealth which constitutes a significant opportunity cost of such policies. It would appear therefore that policies which aim to decrease income inequality are the opposite of those policies that aim at promoting greater efficiency and growth operating on the supply-side of the economy. Whether this is inevitable however, depends to some extent on how widely or narrowly efficiency is defined.

Efficiency in economics is usually defined in terms of the achievement of an optimum allocation of resources which maximises community welfare and the highest output from a given quantity of scarce factor inputs. The former is referred to as allocative efficiency achieved when price is equal to marginal cost and the latter as productive efficiency, when production is at the lowest average cost where marginal cost equals average cost. These two types of efficiency are only guaranteed in perfectly competitive markets in long-run equilibrium. However, there are very few examples of perfectly competitive markets in the real world, so the practical relevance of these efficiency concepts is rather limited. No amount of supply-side policies will convert existing imperfect markets into perfectly competitive markets so policies such as privatisation will not magically achieve allocative or productive efficiency. In the UK for example, the privatisation of the railways in the 1990s does not appear to have achieved any significant efficiency gains and many customers feel that the quality of the service provided has deteriorated while tickets costs have increased. Similarly, there is very little real-world evidence to support the view that increases in the minimum wage do actually cause unemployment to increase and it is possible that the increased spending power of low income earners will actually generate more demand for products and workers. The belief that making income taxes less progressive by reducing the marginal tax rates paid by the highest income earners is often justified by reference to the 'trickle-down effect' which claims that cutting taxes for the wealthy will stimulate increased economic activity and investment that will eventually benefit everyone in the economy. This was in fact used as an argument to support President Trump's decision to cut taxes for millionaires and billionaires. The trickle-down effect, however, does not constitute an economic theory and is disputed by many modern economists, especially those who follow the Keynesian school of thought. It seems more likely that if the equivalent amount of the tax cuts to the wealthy was given to low income groups instead there would be a greater impact on growth in the economy suggesting that the 'trickle up effect' is stronger than the 'trickle-down effect'.

The extent to which making taxation less progressive will have a positive effect on efficiency and growth by stimulating the supply-side of the economy is difficult to judge and the wider implications of income inequality need to be considered as well. Large and increasing disparities in income within and between countries can generate long-term problems that have an effect on both efficiency and growth. By increasing the level of relative poverty, low income families increasingly struggle to fulfil their economic aspirations causing them to become disheartened and pessimistic. Their health suffers and they will become less efficient and contribute less to the performance of the economy. It might also lead to an increase in drug abuse, alcoholism and crime that also represents a reduction in economic efficiency. Sociological studies have shown that a happy workforce with access to a living wage will be more productive than those who are struggling to survive on low minimum wages. Furthermore, various studies, such as that conducted by the OECD in 2015, have shown that increasing income inequality in wealthy countries has reduced potential growth through reduced social mobility and skills acquisition and less access to quality education. The view that large inequalities in income and wealth is damaging to growth and stability in the long-run has also been forcefully argued by the popular French author Thomas Piketty in his book *Capital in the Twenty-First Century* (2013). In addition, increasing income inequality between countries also creates global problems and tensions. Possibly the most significant of these is the growing problem of migration from low-income to high-income countries that many governments are concerned about.

The relationship between income inequality and efficiency and growth is rather complex and cannot be easily analysed with positive economics as many of the views are based on normative beliefs and value judgements, such as the 'trickle-down effect'. It is likely that the belief that the policies needed to reduce income inequality will lead to a sacrifice of efficiency and growth is valid only if a narrow short-term view of efficiency is used. A wider, global, long-term perspective will provide a different conclusion making a balanced objective view difficult to formulate.

This is probably the most difficult topic area of macroeconomics because it incorporates politically motivated policy recommendations with economic theory and normative value judgements. The full complexities of the relationships are outside the scope of IB economics and it is therefore difficult to know where to draw the line between elementary, intermediate and advanced economic theory and analysis. Many of the views expressed by economists are politically motivated and it is very difficult to achieve an objective assessment of the links between progressive taxes and efficiency and more generally the impact of supply-side policies on income distribution and efficiency and growth.

Fortunately, speculative opinions such as those expressed by the Laffer curve have been removed from the syllabus, but the treatment of supply-side policies is in my opinion too simplistic although good well-trained examiners will recognise and give credit for alternative views about their reliability in achieving greater efficiency and growth.

Standard AD/AS diagrams could be used to illustrate short-term and long-term growth associated with supply-side policies and a diagram showing a shift to the right of LRAS would be useful.

2.3 Unit 4 Global Economics

Question 9

(a) Explain two possible causes of an appreciation of a country's currency. [10 marks]

(b) Using real-world examples, discuss the consequences of a rise in a country's exchange rate. [15 marks]

This is a rather typical exchange rate question that could be asked on both the SL and HL paper.

Answer

9 (a) For a currency to appreciate means that it is operating under a system of floating exchange rates whereby the price or value of one country's currency in terms of another currency is determined through the operation of market forces in the foreign exchange market. Like any price, the exchange rate of a currency will be determined by supply and demand so changes in the exchange rate will be caused by changes in either the demand for a currency or the supply of a currency. For an exchange rate to appreciate requires either an increase in the demand for a currency or a decrease in the supply of a currency.

A major determinant of the supply and demand for a currency is the value of the country's trade in goods and services. With respect to such current account transactions the demand for a country's currency reflects the demand for that country's exports while the supply of the currency reflects that country's demand for imports. If a country such as Switzerland has a current account surplus with the value of exports increasing relative to the value of imports, this will cause the demand for the Swiss Franc to increase as shown in diagram 1.

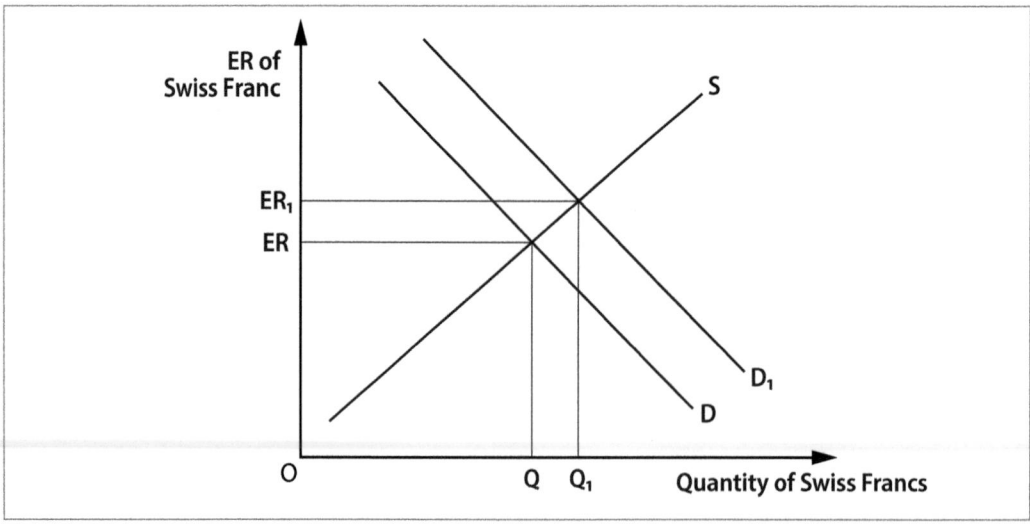

Diagram 1

People wishing to buy goods from Switzerland or wanting to holiday there will need to buy Swiss Francs with their own currency, so the demand for Swiss Francs will increase to D_1 and as a result the currency will appreciate to ER_1.

A second possible cause of an appreciation of a country's currency could be a decrease in the supply of the currency as a result of a decrease in imports. This could occur as a result of a country implementing protectionist policies such as those applied by the USA against China recently. Assuming other things remain equal, this will lead to a decrease in the supply of the currency as shown in diagram 2.

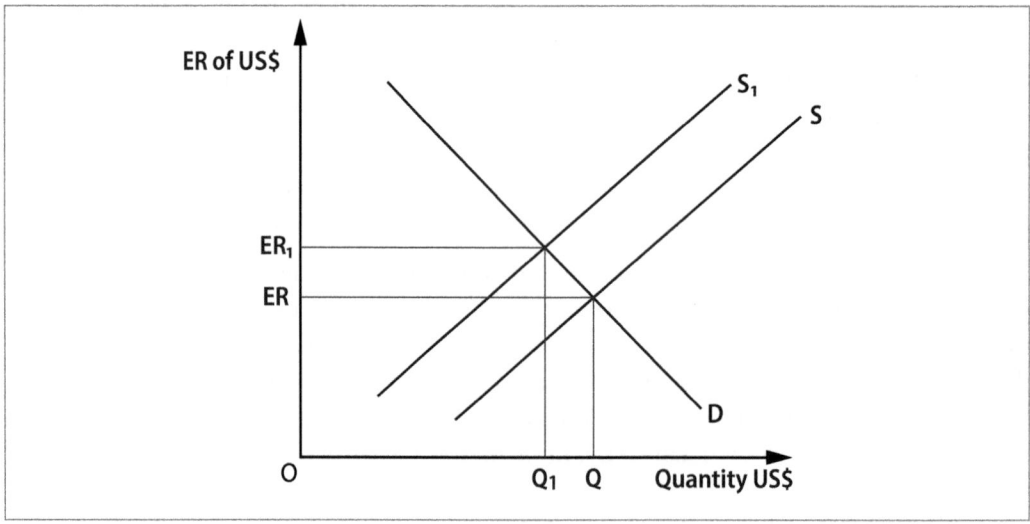

Diagram 2

The decrease in imports leads to the supply of $ shifting to the left to S_1 and as a result the exchange rate appreciates from ER to ER_1. This will only occur however, if there are no other market changes, because it is likely that the implementation of protectionist policies would create concern about the future of global trade and the possibility of a trade war breaking out. In this case speculators are likely to sell the currency which would cause it to depreciate. In practice in the real-world it is very difficult to isolate the factors that influence the exchange rate of a currency as there are many potential influences such as relative interest rates, flows of FDI, government interventions in the foreign exchange markets and a variety of perceptions that can influence speculative buying or selling of currencies.

9 (b) The popular perception of an appreciating currency is that it is good and signifies a dynamic economy performing well. This view is encouraged by the way that such changes are usually described. An appreciation is presented as 'strengthening' and the currency is referred to as a 'strong' currency. Such terms imply advantages and benefits in contrast to the opposite which are described as 'weak' currencies. In the real-world however, these associations do not necessarily apply. Firstly, it will depend on the reason for the appreciation. Switzerland, for example does not regard the frequent appreciation of its currency to be advantageous. The reason is that the appreciation of the Swiss Franc is usually the result of speculative buying in times of economic uncertainty because the currency is viewed as a 'safe haven'. During the Euro crisis 2011-14 the Swiss Franc was consistently high against the Euro and this led the Swiss National Bank to intervene in the foreign exchange market with a large scale selling of Francs in 2014 in order to reduce the exchange rate. Similar interventions took place following the Brexit vote in 2016, and more recently in March 2020 in response to the Coronavirus fears as speculators sold Pounds and Euros and bought Swiss Francs causing the currency to appreciate.

These regular interventions by the Swiss National Bank to combat the currency appreciations are a clear indication that the 'strengthening' of the currency is not considered to be beneficial for the economy. The Swiss economy is very dependent on its export sector including tourism so that any appreciation of the currency will severely affect the competitiveness of these exports. A 10% appreciation of the Swiss Franc against the Euro means that skiing holidays in neighbouring France, Italy and Austria become considerably more attractive than holidays in Switzerland.

An appreciation of a country's currency will have the following sequence of consequences. The first effect will be that the prices of the country's exports will increase, and the prices of imports will decrease by the amount of the appreciation. This will then lead to a decrease in the volume of exports and an increase in the volume of imports. If the demand for exports and imports is elastic the effect will be to decrease export revenues and increase spending on imports. As a result, the current account will face a reduced surplus or an increased deficit and the corresponding decrease in the (X-M) component of AD will cause AD to shift to the left possibly leading to a decrease in growth and an increase in unemployment especially in export industries. Against these negative effects however, we can also identify some positive effects that might occur. The decrease in AD might reduce inflationary pressure if the economy was operating at or near its long-run full employment equilibrium. A further advantage is the possibility that the decrease in import prices might be significant enough to reduce the costs of production for many firms in the economy which would cause the SRAS to shift to the right as shown in diagram 3.

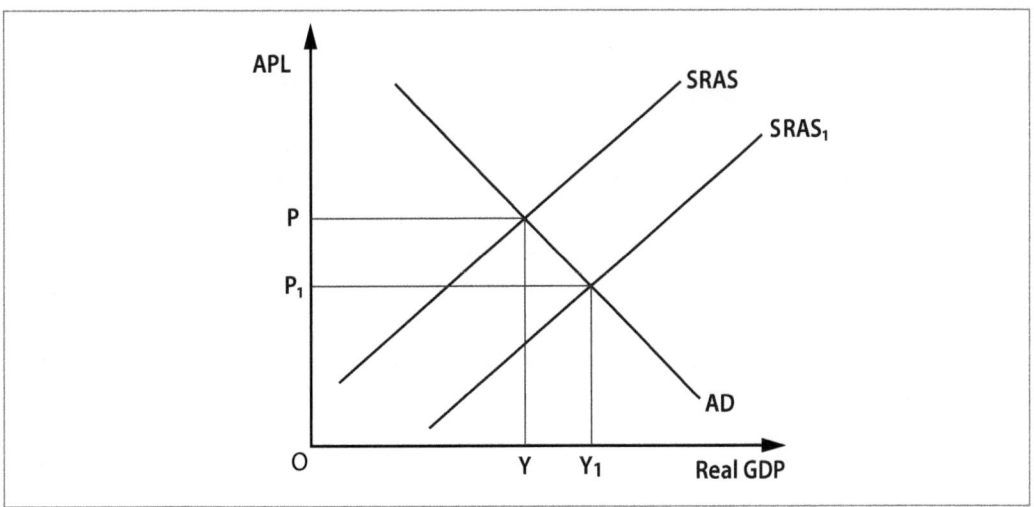

Diagram 3

For a country that imports oil and raw materials the decrease in import prices following an appreciation of the currency will have a positive impact on SRAS which will shift to $SRAS_1$ and as a result real income and employment will increase to Y_1 while at the same time the average price level will fall to P_1 generating a decrease in cost push inflation. The reduction in costs might be large enough to compensate for the higher export prices caused by the initial appreciation of the currency.

It is also possible that the demand for a country's exports is inelastic in which case the effect on the current account and AD will be the opposite of what was described above since export revenues will rise and AD will shift to the right.

A different possible cause of an appreciation of a country's currency is the discovery of oil or natural gas that can lead to what has been called the 'Dutch disease'. The term was originally used by *The Economist* in 1977 to describe the effects on the Dutch economy of the discovery of large deposits of natural gas. The immediate effect was to cause a sharp appreciation of the Dutch Guilder which had a very detrimental effect on the country's non gas manufacturing exports leading to a decline in previously competitive export industries. This effect has also been experienced by countries that have discovered and exploited oil reserves such as Nigeria and Venezuela, and to a lesser extent, the UK with the discovery of North Sea oil from the late 1970s to the early 1980s. Countries that are highly dependent on oil for the majority of their export revenues such as Nigeria and Russia face very volatile exchange rates in response to frequently changing oil prices which can have destabilising effects on their non-oil sectors.

For more balanced economies that are not overdependent on commodity exports an appreciation of the currency would normally reflect a healthy trade balance and/or an attractive destination for inward FDI. In such cases the appreciation would be a reflection of economic strength and potential and would in the long run regulate the rate at which the current account moved into surplus. Ideally, floating exchange rates would moderate the size of current account imbalances but in the real world, this is not always the case as a result of a variety of factors such as trade restrictions, Central Bank manipulation of interest rates and direct interventions in the foreign exchange market as well as speculative buying and selling of currencies.

The consequences of an appreciation of a country's currency are dependent on a variety of factors and will tend to be mixed. Some consequences will be favourable while others will be unfavourable for the stakeholders in the economy. This will depend on the cause of the appreciation and the extent to which the exchange rate reflects the true value of the currency with respect to the country's trade performance and is not being overvalued for other reasons.

On one level this is a fairly straightforward question but the topic of exchange rates is necessarily simplified for IB economics as it is a rather complex topic in real life with many interrelationships and influences. The fact that most commodities are traded in US dollars means that the US dollar is used worldwide as a reserve currency and acts as a benchmark against other currencies. This is a complicating factor which affects the impact of exchange rate changes for commodity exporting countries. As does the IB, I have avoided discussions relating to such complications while at the same time including some relationships that might not be emphasised in a typical HL course of study.

It should also be noted that for any question concerning a currency depreciation, the opposite points would apply in general, although the 'Dutch disease' would not be directly relevant.

Question 10

(a) Explain two ways that a country might try to restrict the freedom of trade. [10 marks]

(b) Using real-world examples discuss the consequences of protectionist trade policies. [15 marks]

Again, a fairly typical question that could appear on either the HL or SL paper.

Answer

10(a) Free trade refers to a global system of international transactions in goods and services between countries without any restrictions in accordance with prices determined in free markets. Restrictions to free trade are referred to as protection and despite the theoretical advantages that free trade confers on countries, many choose to restrict the freedom of trade. There are several ways that a country can interfere with the free movement of trade which aim to bring about a different pattern of trade than would occur under free trade. These restrictions either aim to limit imports or encourage exports. A popular restriction on imports is through the imposition of a tariff which is a tax on imports. The effect of a tariff is shown in diagram 1.

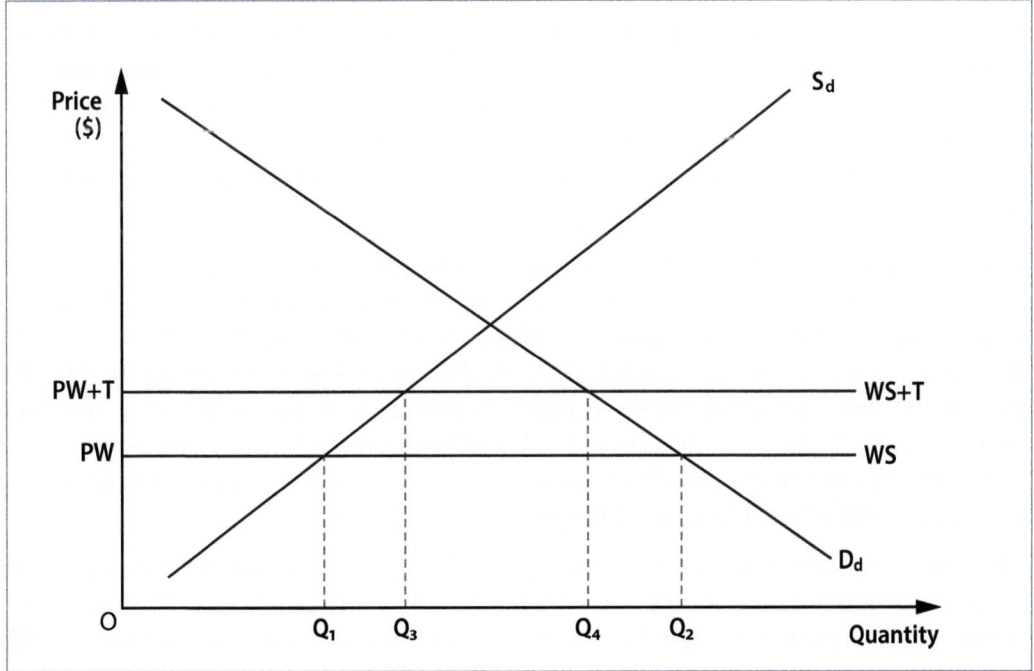

Diagram 1

If a country engages in free trade it will import this product at the word price PW determined by the world supply WS. At this price, the quantity demanded domestically is Q_2 of which Q_1 will be supplied domestically and $Q_1 - Q_2$ will be imported. By imposing a tariff on these imports the world supply will shift to WS+T and the price will increase to PW+T leading to a decrease in imports from $Q_1 - Q_2$ to $Q_3 - Q_4$.

A second way that a country can restrict the freedom of trade is by encouraging a larger volume of exports by providing subsidies to exporters. A subsidy is a payment by the government to a producer that reduces the costs of production leading to a decrease in price and an increase in the quantity produced and consumed. By reducing a producer's costs, a subsidy confers an artificial comparative advantage on the producer allowing them to compete in export markets at a lower opportunity cost. The effect of this is shown in diagram 2.

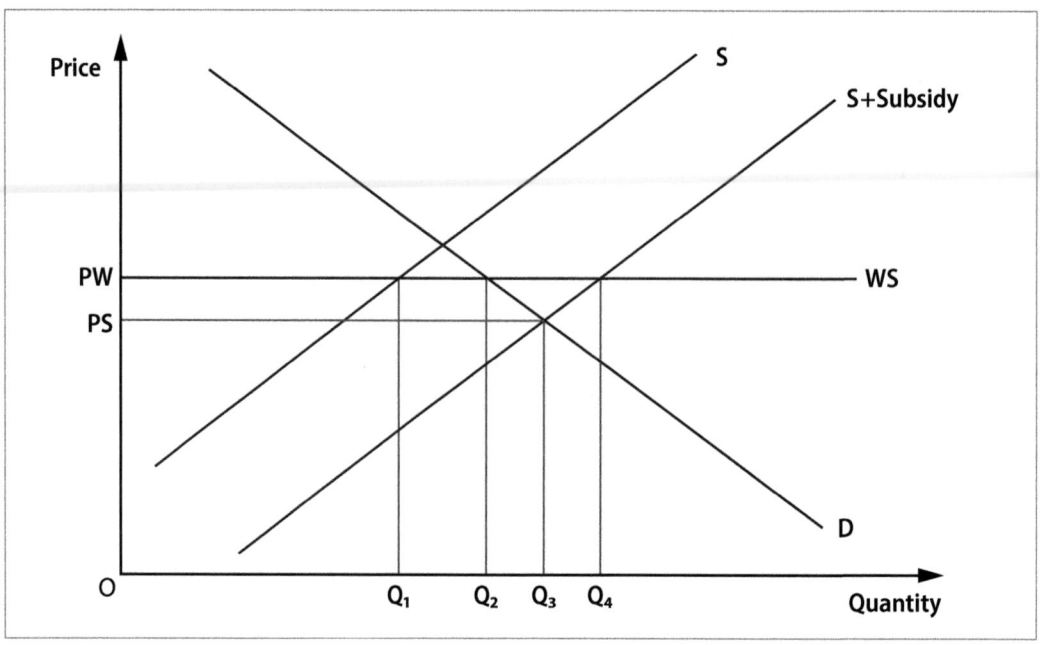

Diagram 2

Without the subsidy this country would be importing $Q_1 - Q_2$ at the world price. With the subsidy however, all the imports would now be replaced by domestic production and the quantity $Q_2 - Q_4$ could now be exported. Alternatively, Q_3 could now be consumed domestically and $Q_3 - Q_4$ could be exported. Either way, the subsidy gives an artificial advantage to the producers and the country is transformed from an importer of this good to an exporter.

10(b) Despite the efforts of the World Trade Organization (WTO) to promote free trade between member countries, there are still a wide range of trade restrictions in place that collectively are described as protection. Until recently, many trade barriers had been broken down and according to the WTO, from 1996 to 2013 an average reduction of 15% in tariffs has been achieved and the volume of trade in goods has quadrupled. However, in recent years the trend towards freer trade has been largely reversed mainly as a result of the protectionist policies that have been introduced by the USA and the retaliation that this has promoted from China and Europe.

The issue of free trade versus protection is complex and involves considerations that go beyond the purely economic aspects of trade based on the application of comparative advantage principles. Although the majority of economists favour free trade and provide convincing economic arguments in support of their views, protectionist policies are quite popular with the average voter. One reason for this is that those who benefit from tariff protection, are highly visible while those who ultimately face the cost of the tariff are much more dispersed and much less visible and are often unaware of the cost to them. In March 2018, President Trump imposed a 25% tariff on imported steel and a 10% tariff on aluminium imports from all countries but temporarily excluding Mexico and Canada. The justification for this move was defined in terms of the strategic importance of these industries as well as accusations that the foreign producers were engaging in unfair competition by subsidising their exports. (You can refer to diagrams in part (a) for the effects of tariffs and subsidies.) The policy was popular in Pennsylvania and other steel producing states where hundreds of jobs for steel workers were highly visibly saved.

The potential negative consequences of this policy were not so visible however, nor were many consequences sufficiently recognised making the policy more popular than objectively it should be. Firstly, those industries which use steel and aluminium as raw materials, like the car industry, faced an increase in their costs of production leading to higher prices and consequently reduced sales and output and job losses. These effects are not immediate and are therefore not initially visible. In addition, consumers now faced with higher prices for many products as a result of the tariffs will have less income to spend on other goods leading to decreased demand for unrelated products that again is not very visible. Another less-visible consequence is the possibility of retaliation by the steel exporting countries with tariffs on American goods. For example, China responded to US tariffs with restrictions on the import of soya beans from America together with a wide range of other products. Since then a variety of protectionist policies and retaliations have occurred leading to what is generally described as a trade war. At the same time, the Trump administration has had to compensate some of the producers affected by the retaliatory policies. For example, in 2019 a $16 billion assistance package was provided to American soya bean farmers. This might resolve the problem faced by American farmers in the short run, but in the long run it is quite likely that they will lose their access to the large Chinese market because China will look to other countries to secure their supplies of soya beans and other products. This could also have unforeseen repercussions on important global issues such as climate change because an alternative source of agricultural imports is Brazil. In order to supply the new Chinese market there will be an increase in the intensity of land clearing involving more rapid destruction of the Amazon rain forest with potentially devastating effects on the climate.

In addition to the jobs and strategic importance arguments, the American President argued that the tariffs were justified because China was a currency manipulator which allowed it to maintain a large current account surplus with the USA. The President claimed that restricting imports from China would solve the US current account deficit problem. Furthermore, the size of the imposed tariffs meant that the USA gained billions of dollars in revenue which could be used to compensate farmers who were affected by the Chinese retaliatory tariffs.

The extent to which these arguments are justified is very difficult to establish partly because the determinants of a country's exchange rate are quite complex (see previous question 9). A counter argument is that the problem is not China preventing its exchange rate from rising but rather that the US$ is overvalued due to the Federal Reserve raising interest rates in 2018 and 2019 together with speculative buying of US$. With respect to the US current account deficit, many economists would argue that the cause is not unfair trading policies employed by China but rather that the US budget deficit which is at historically high levels, generates excess demand in the economy which leads to a higher volume of imports. Protectionist policies will not solve the current account problem because the cause is the overvalued $ and the large budget deficit.

Given the high degree of interdependence between countries in the global economy and the reliance of economies on trade, it is probably true to say that protectionist policies might benefit some sectors of an economy in the short run but that the overall disruption to world trade will have damaging effects on all countries in the long run.

Overall, there is very little economic justification for protectionist policies and their popularity has more to do with nationalism and political agendas than potential economic benefits. A less economically developed country could justify putting tariffs on imported cars for purposes of raising tax revenues which are otherwise difficult to collect, but a rich country like the USA cannot legitimately use this justification. Nor is the argument of strategic importance very convincing since the USA can secure supplies of steel and aluminium from friendly countries such as Canada and the EU. Protectionism, by supporting inefficient industries leads to a loss of productivity and productive efficiency in the long run which will have serious consequences for world growth and potential output.

This turned out to be quite a long answer and there is still a lot that could be included.

For part (a) it would have been possible to select quotas or bureaucratic controls as alternatives, but in my experience most students are not comfortable with the quota diagram and so would prefer the tariff and subsidy diagram. Bureaucratic controls would be the 'lazy' option as there is no diagram that can be suitably used and little that can be said about them.

Part (b) has many alternative real-world examples that can be used, but I have selected the most topical which involves the trade war initiated by the USA with China and other countries. Alternative examples include a discussion of trade creation and trade diversion resulting from the common external tariff that is applied by common markets such as the EU. Development issues could also be introduced in relation to US cotton subsidies and EU sugar subsidies. Any well developed discussion of alternative real-world examples will be rewarded by the examiners, including examples that are used to show the potential benefits of protection for those who want to argue against free trade. It could be argued that sanctions imposed by the EU on Russia have actually benefitted the Russian economy by providing incentives for local industries to develop producing import substitutes and in this way assisting the diversification of the economy away from its overdependence on oil and gas.

Finally, the ongoing repercussions from the spread of the corona-virus pandemic can be used as an example of how over exposure to free trade can lead to risky dependence on imports and provide a potential justification for protectionism to reduce these risks.

Question 11

(a) Explain two barriers to development typically faced by a country with a very low HDI measure. [10 marks]

(b) Using real-world examples evaluate the role of FDI in promoting growth and development for a less economically developed country. [15 marks]

Answer

11(a) HDI is a composite measure of well-being based on income per head, and education and health as indicated by adult literacy, school enrollment and life expectancy. A low HDI therefore indicates a combination of low income, and poor education and health. All ten of the lowest HDI ranked countries in the world are located in sub-Saharan Africa (SSA) and share many common development characteristics. Of the many barriers to development that exist, possibly the two most significant for these low HDI ranking countries are overdependence on a narrow range of primary commodities and lack of adequate health care and education. Both of these barriers contribute to the poverty cycle that these countries are trapped in. Burkina Faso is one of the SSA countries in the lowest ranks of the HDI and faces both of these barriers. Its economy is dependent on cotton and gold which account for over 85% of export revenues and 80% of the working population is engaged in subsistence agriculture. Virtually the entire economy is dependent on the world price of cotton and gold and the volume of production that can be exported. These commodity prices are very volatile as is their output since cotton requires large quantities of water to grow and rainfall is becoming increasingly unreliable in the cotton growing areas. A further problem is the high levels of subsidies given to cotton producers in the USA which tend to depress world prices and prevents Burkina Faso from competing effectively in world markets. The performance of the economy and the rate of growth is therefore determined by the world price of gold and cotton. When prices are high the economy does well, but when prices fall the economy will suffer. This overdependence on risky and unpredictable markets keeps incomes low confining a large proportion of the population to poverty (40% of the population is below the poverty line which defines absolute poverty). This factor of low and unstable income is a contributing factor to the relatively low levels of education and health that keep the country trapped in poverty and perpetuates the low levels of productivity. School enrollment is extremely low in rural areas (40% in primary and 28% in secondary) and although life expectancy has been rising steadily it is still quite low at 61.74 years, up from 56.65 in 2010. To break the poverty cycle one or more of these links need to be improved, but the persistence of low income makes this difficult in practice and would require a significant diversification of the economy. The adult literacy rate is 41% overall and even lower in rural areas and is among the lowest in SSA. This lack of good education and health care combined with low incomes constitute the most significant barriers to growth and development for many of the poorest countries in SSA.

11 (b) Foreign direct investment (FDI) refers to long term, fixed capital investment, mainly by multinational corporations (MNCs) in other countries. It typically involves the MNC setting up a production unit in another country. For example, Apple, an American company, has factories in China that assemble iPhones and over 50% of Nike's products are produced in Vietnam. For countries that are trapped in the poverty cycle of low income-low savings-low investment-low growth, FDI can be an effective means of breaking the cycle. It does this by by-passing the impact that low income and low savings has on investment while at the same time promoting greater diversification of the economy.

Over the past few years, the value of FDI globally has declined (from $1.5 trillion in 2017 to $1.3 trillion in 2018) but FDI in Africa has increased to an estimated $46 billion in 2018 which represents an increase of around 11%. European MNCs are the main sources of FDI in Africa, but China is steadily increasing its presence in Africa. It is undeniable that FDI provides a potential stimulus to growth and development for countries that are trapped in the poverty cycle, but there are increasing concerns regarding the long-term costs of this investment for the host countries.

As outlined in part (a) Burkina Faso could potentially benefit from FDI which in 2019 accounted for almost 20% of GDP. However, the bulk of FDI is in the mining sector and might present a threat to sustainability in the long run. Mining companies in Africa have a very poor reputation for respecting environmental concerns and the local jobs that are provided tend to be exploitative and low paid. In addition, this type of FDI perpetuates the over dependence on risky commodities rather than providing the diversification that would promote a more stable path for growth and development. Rather than relying on volatile revenues from cotton exports it might be a better proposition for Burkina Faso to attract foreign investment in textile manufacturing using the domestically grown cotton to make clothing and other items. Exporting manufactured cotton goods would give much more value added than exporting cotton at world prices depressed by US subsidies. Textile manufacturing would also provide jobs and training for the local population and encourage the transfer of skills and the incentives for future business ventures by local entrepreneurs. As this type of manufacturing develops more people will move out of agricultural production allowing for an increase in labour productivity in the farming sector and a general improvement in productivity and wages all round. Although possibly more environmentally friendly than mining, there is still the danger that manufacturing enterprises can also exploit workers and might also employ children in unhealthy conditions. In such cases any economic growth would be at the expense of development e.g. with children working in factories rather than going to school. In the past many MNCs have been accused of employing children in their overseas factories. For example, in 2007 Gap was found to be retailing garments made in an Indian factory where children as young as 10 were forced to work. Consumer reaction against such reports has led many companies to be more vigilant in order to protect their ethical image, but the practice continues in many cases. A recent report by Amnesty International revealed that nine well known MNCs including Unilever, Nestlé and Procter and Gamble buy palm oil from production units in Indonesia that employ child labour and exploit workers. Whether this form of FDI contributes to long-term development in Indonesia and India is debatable. Only if MNCs are serious about their image of social responsibility and ensure that the workers in their overseas factories are treated fairly and paid a living wage in acceptable working conditions will the FDI contribute to development and not just growth and the enrichment of the factory managers.

FDI is something of a double-edged sword for many countries. On the one hand it promotes growth and jobs and can stimulate economic diversification but on the other hand it can lead to unsustainable environmental destruction and exploitation of children, women and workers in general.

Ethiopia is a good example of this as it has attracted considerable inward FDI from China over the past decade and this has contributed to significant growth at an average of 9% from 2008 to 2018. These economic benefits were widely shared and promoted development with a fall in the country's poverty rate to 31% by 2015. In addition, life expectancy rose from about 52 in 2000 to 66 in 2017, and infant mortality more than halved over that period. Much of the growth is the result of spending on infrastructure financed with loans from China and the World Bank. However, this creates problems of indebtedness for the future which may not be sustainable. Furthermore, many of the manufacturing projects set up by Chinese companies, such as shoe making using locally sourced leather has not had the expected benefits as exports are not significant while imports of cheap Chinese shoes have soared. The Chinese shoe companies have squeezed the local producers out of the market by buying up all the leather and making the domestic market dependent on imports.

With respect to growth, the weight of evidence suggests that FDI is a major contributory factor and the high growth rates experienced by many SSA countries like Ethiopia are due to inward FDI, especially from China. However, the positive impact of FDI on sustainable development is more difficult to determine as there are serious environmental, social and cultural concerns related to the changes it imposes on the host nations. This is especially true of FDI in mineral extraction but also with manufacturing enterprises that might abuse labour and exploit children. FDI is an important means for breaking the poverty cycle and promoting necessary diversification of the economy, but there will always be an opportunity cost involved that is difficult to calculate accurately.

Again this turned out be a rather long answer but with many additional points that could have been mentioned depending on the wide range of real-world examples that are available. A more analytical approach could also be taken using macroeconomic analysis and diagrams showing the demand side and supply side impact of FDI which will shift both AD and LRAS to the right. There are plenty of examples of environmental damage as a result of FDI for oil extraction in Nigeria and mining in the DRC as well as abuse of workers in sweatshops throughout Asia working for Western fashion brands. A different collection of examples would allow for other factors to be considered such as whether the FDI increases exports or simply leads to more imports or whether it creates jobs for locals or if foreign workers are used. As long as relevant real-world examples are used and discussed, a good answer can be provided without the need to cover every single aspect.

Question 12

(a) Explain two reasons why aid might not be beneficial for the recipient country. [10 marks]

(b) Using real-world examples discuss the extent to which fair trade and micro credit schemes can effectively promote development in less economically developed countries. [15 marks]

Answer

12 (a) Until recently, aid was generally considered to be essential to assist poor countries in their fight against poverty and its related problems. However, after decades of aid amounting to billions of dollars, many of the recipient countries have remained trapped in the poverty cycle. This has led to a serious questioning of the long-term effectiveness of aid and some economists have even suggested that aid actually perpetuates the problem of poverty rather than solving it. This view was most prominently popularised by the Zambian economist and former consultant for the World Bank, Dambisa Moyo in her book *Dead Aid* published in 2009. Referring mainly to aid received by African countries she concludes that not only has charitable aid been ineffective, but that it has actually been counter-productive making the problem worse.

There are two main reasons for this. The first is that it creates a dependency that erodes initiative and incentives for self-improvement and the second is that it promotes corruption and the diverting of funds for personal gain of politicians and public officials. In order to explain these issues it is first necessary to identify the different types of aid. Moyo distinguishes three main types: humanitarian or emergency aid; charity-based aid mainly distributed by NGOs; and systematic aid either bilateral from government to government or multilateral via institutions such as the World Bank. Of these three types it is the last that is by far the largest and potentially the most damaging. However, even emergency and charitable aid can be counter-productive and damaging to the economy of the country receiving it. For example, well-meaning charities often mobilise the distribution of free food to alleviate starvation in countries that are afflicted by drought and famine. The problem is that when free food is available, nobody will buy any of the locally produced food so local farmers who managed to produce some of their crops are unable to sell and will have no income to buy necessary seeds and equipment for the next season thus effectively destroying future agricultural production. A similar example is the distribution of free malaria nets by charities. These will help prevent a deadly disease but, the local mosquito net producers will be driven out of business leading to job losses and increased poverty for the owners and workers and their dependents. Such problems could however, be avoided if the aid agencies first bought up all the local produce and then distributed it free with their own supplies.

The potentially most damaging type of aid is the systematic bilateral aid from government to government which as well as promoting corruption and dependence also serves the interests of the donor countries which are able to exert political influence on the recipients. Far from reducing poverty, this aid has coincided with an increase in poverty. Between 1970 and 1998 when aid flows were at their peak, poverty in Africa increased from 11% to 66%. By fuelling corruption, aid undermines the efficient working of the economy and discourages foreign investment leading to lower growth and increased poverty. According to Moyo, the main beneficiaries of this type of aid are the political leaders who have siphoned off $billions into Swiss bank accounts.

Apart from corruption, this type of aid leads to a dependency and the removal of incentives to promote other more productive sources of revenue. Without aid, countries would be obliged to collect revenue from taxes which in turn would require more effective programs for income creation. Governments would be obliged to promote growth and trade and to encourage FDI rather than waiting for the next dose of aid like an addict.

12(b) Fair trade and micro credit schemes are popularly seen as effective ways of promoting growth and development in LEDCs by targeting the poorer sections of the economy and providing incentives for enterprise in contrast to aid which can have a disincentive effect, as outlined in part (a). Fair trade is a scheme intended to provide producers with a guaranteed price for their products and to ensure more sustainable and equitable trade relations. It now covers many products ranging from handicrafts and textiles to a wide range of agricultural goods such as tea, coffee and cocoa. It attempts to address the problem faced by many LEDCs that rely on a narrow range of commodity exports, of volatile and unpredictable prices. Fair trade prices will often be higher than market prices and will therefore guarantee a more stable income for producers. Many companies in developed countries have adopted fair trade using it as an ethical trading selling point. In the UK the major supermarkets are keen to promote their fair trade credentials as are many coffee retailers such as Starbucks. Consumers in developed countries are on the whole willing to pay higher prices for fair trade certified products in the belief that they are supporting poor farmers and communities in LEDCs. The extent to which fair trade does actually benefit the farmers and agricultural communities and promote growth and development is difficult to assess however. In a recent study of fair trade cocoa in the Ivory Coast by Eva-Marie Meemken, an agricultural economist, she found that farmers who participated in the scheme were better off than those that did not, but there was no advantage for the workers who harvested the cocoa. This indicates that the overall benefits of the scheme could be limited to the farm owners rather than to the wider community. An additional factor that has been pointed out by some economists is that by interfering with the market mechanism, fair trade prices encourage the production of crops that are becoming less profitable and reduce the incentives for farmers to follow the market price signals and switch to cultivating more profitable crops. In this way over-specialisation in a narrow range of commodity production is encouraged which works against the desired diversification of economic activity. Fair trade is increasingly being seen as something that benefits the Western supermarkets and MNCs rather than the farm workers and the poor communities in which they operate.

Micro-credit schemes were also for many years seen as a major potential contributor to growth and development as a result of some initial success stories. However, like fair trade these schemes have also been more closely looked at recently and as a result there is now a bit less optimism about how effectively they can promote growth and development.

These schemes were pioneered by the Grameen Bank, set up by Muhammad Yunus in Bangladesh in 1983 and have subsequently spread throughout the world in various forms. They provide small loans to individuals who would not be able to secure a loan from a traditional bank, to assist them in setting up a small business or venture. Without any physical capital to offer as collateral, poor people have no access to credit facilities and micro credit or finance has helped to fill this gap and encourage entrepreneurial activity in low income communities such as villages in Asia or Africa. An example might be a woman taking out a loan of $20 to buy pots and pans in which to cook food that can be sold in the local market, or using the small loan to buy a sewing machine that can be used to make clothes for sale in a street market. If successful, these schemes can promote growth and development in the local community, but on a small scale. The problem is that the ventures are not always successful and the interest rates charged on the loans are usually quite high and can lead to severe debt problems. In an article in the *Guardian* newspaper in 2013, it was reported that the widespread use of micro credit in South Africa had had no positive impact on growth and development and on the contrary had led to a debt problem for the poor who were forced to sell any assets they possessed to pay back their loans. The type of small scale businesses that the loans were used for already existed and so rather than filling a gap in the market, they simply reduced the market share of all producers. In practice it is very difficult for the small enterprises that are financed by the micro credit loans to ensure a return large enough to cover the interest repayments on the loans.

In individual cases, micro credit can have a positive effect and it has been especially useful in promoting the empowerment of women in some communities, because women are given preference as recipients of loans due to their greater commitment to repayment and efficient use of the loans. However, long-term studies have found little evidence that, in countries such as India and Bangladesh where $billions have been provided in micro credit, there has been any significant reduction in poverty as a result. Schemes that create jobs have a much greater positive impact on growth and development and poverty reduction. A large loan to an enterprising entrepreneur to set up a textile factory that employs 100 workers will have a greater positive impact on the local economy than giving small loans to 100 individuals to buy sewing machines to make clothes.

Both fair trade and micro credit can have a positive effect on growth and development, but it would be wrong to exaggerate their potential impact. It is not likely that either of these schemes will have a significant effect and certainly not as much as FDI for example.

ECONOMICS SL&HL: PRACTICE QUESTIONS FOR PAPERS 1 & 2

Chapter 3: Introduction to paper 2

For the new syllabus in Economics applying to examinations from May 2022, paper 2 has undergone significant changes which you should bear in mind if you find past papers for prior years. It is still a data response paper including both text and data, but the questions are longer and are based on more data.

You are now:

- required to answer one question from a choice of two;
- allowed 1 hour and 45 minutes to complete the paper.

The questions may be taken from all four units of the syllabus.

3.1 General points

The questions are each subdivided into seven parts, (a), (b), (c), (d), (e), (f) and (g). Parts (a) and (b) both have subparts showing (i) and (ii)

The allocation of marks per part are:

Question part	Maximum marks
(a)	4 marks divided between (i) and (ii) with 2 marks each
(b)	5 marks divided between (i) and (ii) with 3 marks for one part and 2 marks for the other
(c) to (f)	4 marks each
(g)	15 marks
Total	40 marks (same for HL and SL)

Paper 2 counts for 30% of the total marks for HL, and 40% of the total for SL. It is likely that the same texts/data will be used for both SL and HL, but the questions set may be different to reflect the syllabus differences in the requirements for SL and HL.

Part (a) will normally require 2 definitions; part (b) will normally require calculations and/or a diagram; parts (c) to (f) will require diagrams to explain issues raised in the text/data and part (g) will require a discussion or evaluation using information from the text/data and your knowledge of economics. Part (g) accounts for 37.5% of the total marks for the paper and you should spend at least 40 minutes on your answer to this part. You should be able to answer parts (a) to (f) in less than 65 minutes giving you extra time for part (g).

3. INTRODUCTION TO PAPER 2

3.2 Assessment criteria

Each question will normally have 3 texts together with 1 or 2 tables which present economic/development data for a country.

For part (a) the definitions need to be precise and concise. One sentence should normally be adequate. For part (b) questions the calculations should include some indication of method or formula and answers should be expressed to 2 decimal places.

For parts (c) to (f) the diagrams need to be clearly and accurately drawn, fully labelled and described with a clear reason provided for what the diagram is explaining.

For part (g) the following guidelines apply:

Marks	Level descriptor
0	• The work does not reach a standard described by the descriptors below.
1–3	• The response indicates little understanding of the specific demands of the question. • Economic theory is stated but it is not relevant. • Economic terms are stated but they are not relevant. • The response contains no evidence of synthesis or evaluation. • A real-world example(s) is identified but it is irrelevant.
4–6	• The response indicates some understanding of the specific demands of the question. • Relevant economic theory is described. • Some relevant economic terms are included. • The response contains evidence of superficial synthesis or evaluation. • A relevant real-world example(s) is identified.
7–9	• The response indicates understanding of the specific demands of the question, but these demands are only partially addressed. • Relevant economic theory is partly explained. • Some relevant economic terms are used appropriately. • Where appropriate, relevant diagram(s) are included. • The response contains evidence of appropriate synthesis or evaluation but lacks balance. • A relevant real-world example(s) is identified and partly developed in the context of the question.
10–12	• The specific demands of the question are understood and addressed. • Relevant economic theory is explained. • Relevant economic terms are used mostly appropriately. • Where appropriate, relevant diagram(s) are included and explained. • The response contains evidence of appropriate synthesis or evaluation that is mostly balanced. • A relevant real-world example(s) is identified and developed in the context of the question.
13–15	• The specific demands of the question are understood and addressed. • Relevant economic theory is fully explained. • Relevant economic terms are used appropriately throughout the response. • Where appropriate, relevant diagram(s) are included and fully explained. • The response contains evidence of effective and balanced synthesis or evaluation. • A relevant real-world example(s) is identified and fully developed to support the argument.

ECONOMICS SL&HL: PRACTICE QUESTIONS FOR PAPERS 1 & 2

Chapter 4: Paper 2 practice questions

The specimen exam paper available at the time of writing suggests that the questions will cover all areas of the syllabus, including development, so knowledge of all possible diagrams and definitions is essential.

The following are representative of the texts and data that will be included in the exam questions together with appropriate answers.

Question 1

Read the extracts and answer the questions that follow.

> ### Text A — Overview of Kenya
>
> (1) In 2019, Kenya's **economic growth** averaged 5.7%, placing Kenya as one of the fastest growing economies in Sub-Saharan Africa. The recent economic expansion has been boosted by a stable macroeconomic environment, positive investor confidence and a resilient services sector.
>
> (2) Kenya's economy is being hit hard through supply and demand shocks on external and domestic fronts, interrupting its recent broad-based growth path. Apart from the COVID-19 (coronavirus) pandemic, the locust* attack which started early 2020, has affected many parts of Kenya especially the North East. It has had a negative impact on the food security and growth of the agriculture sector in the country.
>
> (3) Real gross domestic product (GDP) growth is projected to decelerate from an annual average of 5.7% (2015-2019) to 1.5% in 2020. However, if it takes longer than expected to bring the COVID-19 pandemic under control, GDP could contract by 1.0% in 2020, and see a delay in the projected recovery to 5.2% growth in 2021. The downside risks include a protracted global **recession** undermining Kenya's export, tourism and remittance inflows, further tightening of COVID-19 health response measures that disrupt the domestic economic activity, fiscal slippages and weather-related shocks.
>
> (4) World Bank support to Kenya's pandemic response includes emergency funding to strengthen medical services and reduce the spread of the virus, as well as budget support to help close the fiscal financing gap while supporting reforms that help advance the government's inclusive growth agenda.
>
> (5) In addition to aligning the country's long-term development agenda to Vision 2030, the President outlined the "Big Four" development priority areas for his final term as President prioritising manufacturing, universal healthcare, affordable housing and food security.
>
> *locust: Insect that eats agricultural food crops

4. PAPER 2 PRACTICE QUESTIONS

Text B — Coronavirus impact in Kenya

(1) The economic and social disruptions induced by the COVID-19 (coronavirus disease 2019) pandemic have eroded progress in poverty reduction in Kenya, forcing an estimated two million more Kenyans into poverty.

(2) Using data to track the impact of the crisis on firms and households, the 22nd edition of the Kenya Economic Update, Navigating the Pandemic, finds that the pandemic and measures to mitigate the spread of the virus are creating multiple challenges for Kenya's private sector, with severe consequences for household jobs and incomes.

(3) "COVID-19 poses an unprecedented shock to the economy, disrupting economic activity," said Keith Hansen, World Bank Country Director for Kenya. "The government, with the help of partners, needs to ensure that the shock remains temporary, by targeting support to the most vulnerable affected households."

(4) The negative impact of COVID-19 on the private sector has trickled down to household welfare via reduced job opportunities and lower earnings. Unemployment has almost doubled compared to its pre-COVID level. Wage workers–and especially women–who are still employed face a reduction in working hours and earnings. Almost 1 in 3 household-run businesses are not operating currently, with revenues decreasing across all sectors. Remittances have fallen, and few households have benefitted from direct cash assistance. Youth are also negatively affected by the pandemic, with revenues and profits strongly reduced for micro-enterprises run by young entrepreneurs, with only few of them making use of government and non-governmental organisations (NGO) support programs.

Text C — Kenya Cuts Key Rate to 7%

(1) The Central Bank of Kenya has for the fourth time since November 2020 cut the benchmark interest rate to 7% which is its lowest rate for ten years. The aim is to provide a necessary stimulus to the economy which is suffering from the economic disruption caused by the recent pandemic.

Table 1: Economic Data for Kenya

	2017 Data	2019 Data
Population (millions)	46.7	49.4
GDP ($US Billions)	78.7	95.3
Inflation (CPI) %	8	5.1
Current Account %GDP	−6.2	−5
Budget Surplus+/Deficit− as % GDP	−9	−7.6
Interest Rate%	10	8.5
GDP per capita (PPP)	$3,500	$3,600
% of Labour force employed in agriculture	67	65

ECONOMICS SL&HL: PRACTICE QUESTIONS FOR PAPERS 1 & 2

Table 2: Development Data for Kenya

	Previous Data	2019 Data
Human Development Index (HDI)	0.587 (2015)	0.601
Gini index	0.427 (2017)	0.416 (2018)
Life expectancy	62.92 (2015)	66.44
Adult Literacy	78.73 (2014)	81.54 (2018)
% Population below poverty line	46.8 (2006)	36.1 (2016)

(Source: www.worldbank.org)

Questions:

(a) (i) Define the term **economic growth** indicated in bold (Text A, paragraph 1). [2 marks]

(ii) Define the term **recession** indicated in bold (Text A, paragraph 3). [2 marks]

(b) (i) Using information from Table 1, calculate the GDP per capita in 2019. [2 marks]

(ii) Draw a demand and supply diagram to show the impact on food prices of the locust attack in 2020 (Text A, paragraph 2). [3 marks]

(c) Using an AD/AS diagram explain the impact on Kenya's growth of the 'demand shock' (Text A, paragraph 2). [4 marks]

(d) Using an AD/AS diagram explain the supply side impact on the Kenyan economy of the coronavirus pandemic described in Text B. [4 marks]

(e) Using an exchange rate diagram explain the likely impact of the interest rate cuts on the exchange rate of Kenya's currency (Text C). [4 marks]

(f) Using a Lorenz curve diagram explain the impact on the distribution of income in Kenya from 2017 to 2018 as a result of the change in the Gini index (Table 2) [4 marks]

(g) Using information from the text/data and your knowledge of economics, discuss policies that the Kenyan government could implement in order to reduce the negative impact of the pandemic on growth and development. [15 marks]

Answers:

The following answers for questions (a) to (f) would be expected to gain full marks while the answer for question (g) would be expected to be in the top 13–15 mark range. For long questions it is difficult to secure full marks even if all the requisites of the mark scheme are provided as examiners are reluctant to commit to 15/15 in case they are thought to be too generous. For practical purposes 13/14 out of 15 is about the highest mark that you can expect.

(a) (i) Economic growth is a measure of changes in real GDP over time expressed as a percentage.

(ii) A recession corresponds to a downturn in the trade cycle and is characterised by at least two consecutive quarters of negative economic growth.

(b) **(i)** GDP per capita = GDP/population = $95.3 billion/49.4 million

= $1,929.15

(ii) The locust attack will cause the devastation of many food crops such as corn which means that the supply of these crops will be greatly reduced as shown in the following diagram with supply shifting from S to S_1. As a result, the price will increase to P_1.

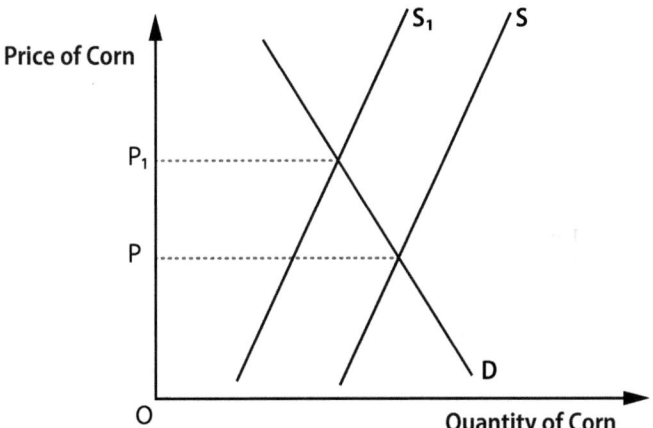

(c) The demand shock refers to a sudden decrease in aggregate demand (AD) caused by the economic disruption to growth in light of the Covid pandemic. This is reflected by a shift in AD to the left from AD to AD_1 and as a result there will be a decrease in real GDP from Y to Y_1 and a fall in the average price level from P to P_1 as shown in the following diagram.

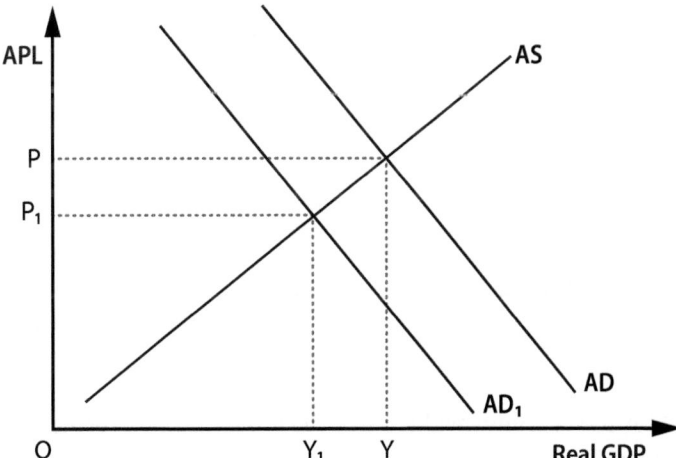

(d) According to Text B the virus has caused a shock to the economy which will affect the supply side by reducing the quantity and quality of the factors of production such as entrepreneurs who will be forced out of business. In addition, the ill health and deaths caused by the virus will reduce the quantity and productivity of labour.

This has the effect of shifting the long-run aggregate supply to the left from LRAS to $LRAS_1$ which causes real GDP to fall from Y_f to Y_{f1} and the average price level to increase from P to P_1 as shown in the following diagram.

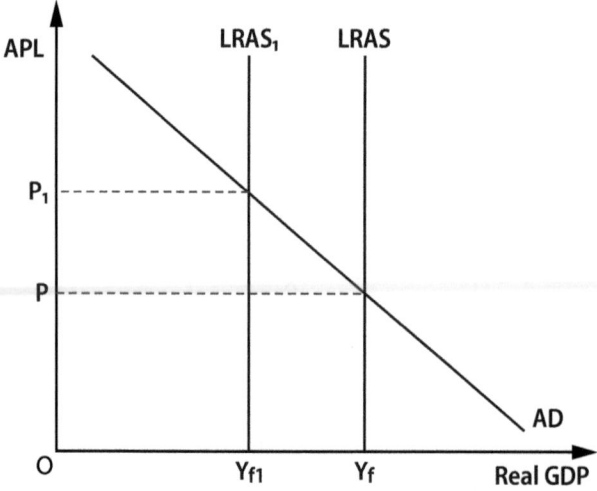

(e) A cut in interest rates will make Kenyan financial assets less attractive as they will now have a lower return so the demand for the Kenyan currency will fall as shown in the following diagram.

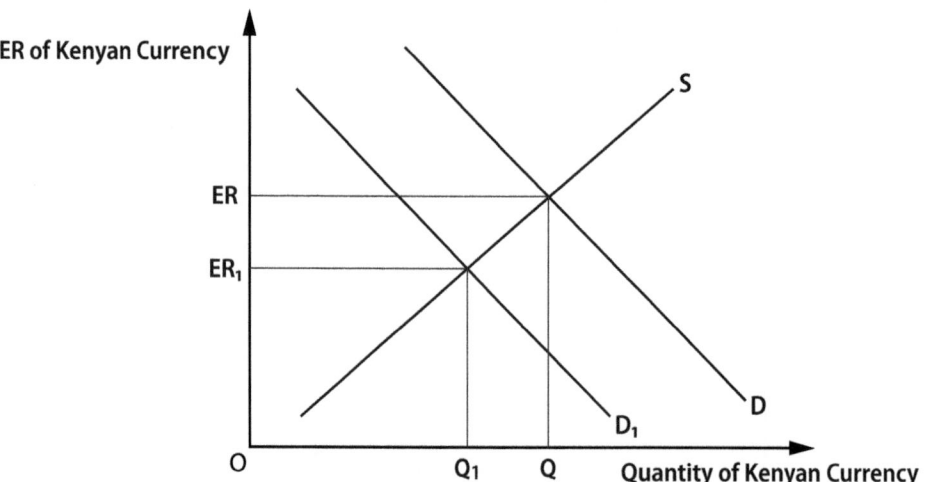

The demand for the currency will fall from D to D_1 and as a result the exchange rate will depreciate to ER_1.

(f) Since the Gini index has decreased from 0.427 to 0.416 it means that the distribution of income has become more equal which is indicated in the diagram below by the shift in the Lorenz curve from A to B towards the 45° line of perfect equality.

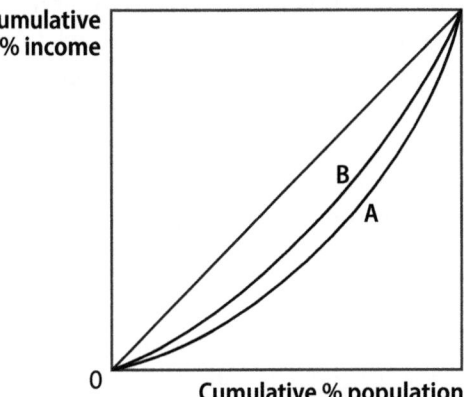

(g) As stated in Text A paragraph 1 Kenya's economy was performing well up to the outbreak of the pandemic with an average growth of 5.7% which was among the highest in Africa. These high growth rates were expected to continue, but as stated in paragraph 3 the projections are now that growth will decelerate to 1.5% with a possibility that "GDP could contract by 1% in 2020". This will also have a negative impact on development since incomes will fall and there will be less ability to invest in health care and education.

The ability of the Kenyan government to reduce the negative impact of the pandemic on growth and development is likely to be constrained by a variety of factors a major one being the fact that the source of the problem is external and therefore outside the scope of any domestic policy measures. As noted in paragraph 3, the global recession will undermine Kenya's foreign currency earnings from exports, tourism and remittances. This reduction in exports will have a significant impact on aggregate demand which will contract leading to a decrease in real GDP as shown in the answer to part (c).

Under normal circumstances the cut in interest rates identified in Text C would be an effective policy for stimulating domestic demand and its effect on the exchange rate as shown in part (e) would be expected to give a boost to exports as they become more competitive. However, the pandemic will not allow any increase in tourism despite the depreciation of the currency and lockdown restrictions will prevent Kenyan workers abroad from earning and sending remittances. The global recession will also depress the demand for Kenyan exports and lower domestic interest rates will not be able to stimulate demand because the pandemic is expected to erode "progress in poverty reduction in Kenya, forcing an estimated two million more Kenyans into poverty." (Text B paragraph 1).

Monetary policy is unlikely to be effective in reversing the deflationary effects of the pandemic and a more direct and active government spending program is a better alternative. The problem is that such an extensive fiscal expansion necessary to supplement domestic demand at a time when unemployment has doubled, and earnings are falling requires access to funds that are not readily available. According to the World Bank, "The government, with the help of partners, needs to ensure that the shock remains temporary, by targeting support to the most vulnerable affected households." However, there is no indication that there will be sufficient aid and foreign assistance to finance such spending. As Table 1 clearly shows, the existing budget deficit at 7.6% of GDP is already quite large as is the current account deficit at 5% of GDP. These imbalances impose a major limitation on the government's ability to spend its way out of the recession.

The impact of the pandemic on growth is hoped to be temporary, but its effect on development could be more permanent. Increased poverty will force some families to take their children out of school and this lost education will not be easy to overcome. In addition, there could be permanent health damage that will further reduce welfare and development. As noted in Text B paragraph 4, women will be particularly adversely affected both economically and socially. Whether the World Bank's support through emergency funding will be sufficient to compensate for the upheaval caused by the pandemic remains to be seen.

Table 2 shows that Kenya has achieved significant improvements in recent years in life expectancy and adult literacy which explains the increase in the HDI but over one third of the population is still below the poverty line and with the expected additional 2 million this % will increase. It is important therefore that the government does not sacrifice its development goals of universal healthcare and food security (Text A paragraph 5) as these will be essential for the achievement of development objectives which are being threatened by the current situation. In order to keep the country on track with its growth and development successes, the Kenyan government needs to engage in a targeted spending program aimed at maintaining income levels for the poorest families, and especially those who have lost their jobs. Health care spending needs to be increased in order to reduce the devastation caused by the pandemic and education should be encouraged and facilitated to guarantee future productivity and prosperity. In addition, the government should provide support and encouragement to small businesses to guarantee their survival as these affect many households and their incomes. By taking a proactive position the government can show its intent and commitment which will encourage foreign direct investment as well as the support of the World Bank and other aid agencies.

In the short run some market-based supply side policies might be able to provide incentives for business enterprise but interventionist policies are not likely to be effective in the short run. What is most urgently required is a large fiscal boost to domestic demand together with a development strategy to ensure that health and education do not suffer.

Part (g) is the most important and most difficult and you will be expected to write a long answer. It is important to make sure that you refer to all 3 texts and both tables. The specimen paper indicates that the whole range of syllabus material will be tested, and you are expected to be able to distinguish between growth and development. Although not mentioned in the specimen mark schemes you might want to include some references to the nine key concepts that have been introduced to the new syllabus as well as a reference to nudge theory if you consider this to be a relevant aspect of government policy. You are not expected to cover every single relevant point but as long as a broad range is covered, and you present a balanced analysis and discussion you should be able to secure high marks. You can refer to diagrams that have been used in previous answers (c) to (f) to support points and you might want to show off your knowledge of economics with a new diagram. For example, in the above answer a poverty cycle diagram could have been added to show the impact of the pandemic on poverty. As long as you display a sound understanding of the differences between growth and development together with the ability to identify and analyse suitable policies with adequate references to the text/data you will gain marks.

Question 2

Read the extracts and answer the questions that follow.

Text A — Overview of Turkey

(1) As a result of the global meltdown resulting from the effect of COVID-19 Turkey's GDP contracted 10 percent in the second quarter of 2020. The contraction for the whole year is likely to be less than this depending on the success of the measures taken to reduce the impact.

(2) Having achieved a surplus last year, the **current account** plunged back into a deficit as exports were decimated. The deficit amounted to US$20 billion (3.4 percent of GDP) in the first half of 2020 as exports fell 21% year on year while imports declined only by 4 percent.

(3) In response to the COVID-19 shock, the authorities resorted to aggressive monetary loosening. Policy interest rates, falling since mid-2019, turned negative in real terms. The Central Bank used several liquidity measures to boost the money supply. A targeted fiscal expansion supported furloughed workers, firms, households, and health services, with the 12-month central government deficit reaching 3.4 percent of GDP in June.

(4) Global uncertainty and domestic monetary loosening led to steady capital outflows, amounting to more than US$20 billion (net) between March and June. These were offset by an additional US$10 billion swap line with the Qatar Central Bank and the use of Central Bank reserves. Even so, the Turkish lira depreciated by 29 percent against the US dollar between January and the end of August. The loose monetary stance and depreciation contributed to the persistence of high **inflation**, which reached 11.8 percent year on year in August.

Text B — Covid-19 and Tourism in Turkey

(1) 2019 was a record year for tourism in Turkey as it attracted more than 45 million foreign visitors. The high season is the summer when 6–7 million visitors per month arrive mainly from Europe, Russia and the Middle East. For most years over the last decade, Turkey has attracted more than 30 million visitors per year which has provided a much-needed source of hard currency income.

(2) In 2019, income from tourism totalled more than US$34 billion, with an average USD 30 billion per annum over the last three years. Without these high tourist revenues, the Turkish current account deficit would be unsustainable.

(3) The collapse of tourism due to travel restrictions in line with health risks is a major reason for the increased current account deficit which is exerting heightened pressure on an already weak currency.

Text C — US Tariffs on Turkish Steel

(1) In August 2018, President Trump decided to increase tariffs on steel imported from Turkey to 50% which some analysts considered to be politically motivated rather than for economic reasons. These were subsequently lowered to 25% in May 2019 partly because steel imports from Turkey had fallen sufficiently.

(2) In June 2018, after the initial imposition of steel tariffs, Turkey decided to retaliate by imposing tariffs on US$ 791 million of imports from the US. The WTO is currently examining the respective arguments to justify these trade restrictions presented by the US and Turkey.

Table 1: Economic Data for Turkey

	2017 Data	2019 Data
Population (millions)	80.8	83.0
GDP (US$ billions)	853	754
Inflation (CPI) %	11.1	15.2
Unemployment %	10.9	13.7
Budget Surplus+/Deficit– as % GDP	–1.5	–2.9
Interest Rate %	8	12
Exchange rate vs US$	3.79	5.75
Domestic demand (% Change)	7.2	–1.4

Table 2: Development Data for Turkey

	Previous Data	2018 Data
Human Development Index (HDI)	0.8 (2015)	0.82 (2020)
Gini index	0.414 (2017)	0.419
Life expectancy	76.17 (2015)	77.44
Adult Literacy	95.6 (2015)	96.15 (2017)

(Source: www.worldbank.org)

Questions:

(a) (i) Define the term **current account** indicated in bold (Text A, paragraph 2). [2 marks]

(ii) Define the term **inflation** indicated in bold (Text A, paragraph 4). [2 marks]

(b) (i) Using information from Table 1, calculate the % increase in unemployment from 2017 to 2019. [2 marks]

(ii) Draw a trade cycle diagram and indicate where the Turkish economy is currently situated (Text A, paragraph 1). [3 marks]

4. PAPER 2 PRACTICE QUESTIONS

(c) Using a money market diagram explain the impact of the increased money supply on Turkish interest rates described in Text A, paragraph 3. [4 marks]

(d) Using an AD/AS diagram explain the impact of the increased current account deficit on the Turkish economy described in (Text B, paragraph 3). [4 marks]

(e) Using an appropriate diagram explain the likely impact of the steel tariffs on the volume of steel imports from Turkey entering the US (Text C, paragraph 1). [4 marks]

(f) Using a PPC diagram explain the impact on the Turkish economy as a result of the change in the life expectancy and adult literacy (Table 2) [4 marks]

(g) Using information from the text/data and your knowledge of economics, discuss policies that the Turkish government could implement in order to reduce the current account deficit. [15 marks]

Answers:

(a) (i) Current account is a record of the value of a country's exports and imports of goods and services together with income flows and transfers.

(ii) Inflation is a persistent increase in the average price level over time

(b) (i) Unemployment increased from 10.9% to 13.7% so the increase is

$$2.8/10.9 \times 100 = 25.69\%$$

(ii) The Turkish economy is in the recession phase of the cycle at C.

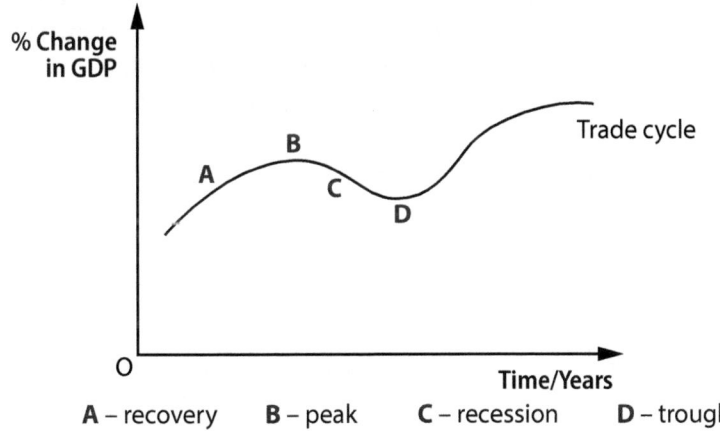

A – recovery   B – peak   C – recession   D – trough

(c)

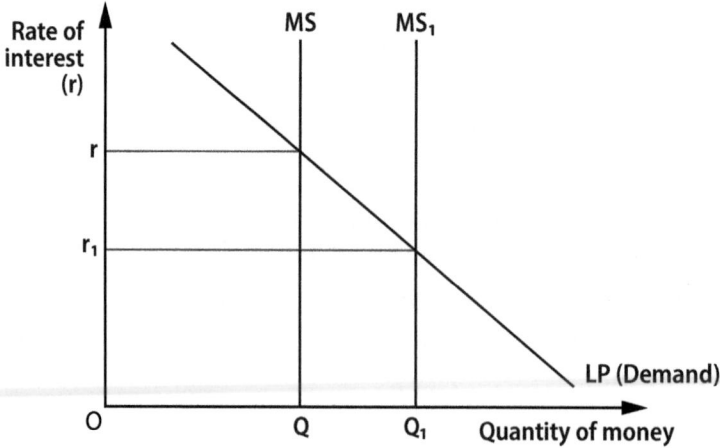

The money market is where the equilibrium rate of interest is established where the money supply (MS) is equal to the demand for money to hold, known as liquidity preference (LP).

The aggressive monetary loosening referred to means that the Central Bank increased the money supply represented by the increase from MS to MS_1 and as a result of this the equilibrium rate of interest falls from r to r_1.

(d) The increased current account deficit means that the value of imports and outflows is greater than the value of exports and inflows and other things being equal, this will lead to a fall in the (X - M) component of AD. This is shown in the diagram with the shift in AD to AD_1 and as a result there will be a fall in both the level of output from Y to Y_1 and a fall in the average price level from P to P_1.

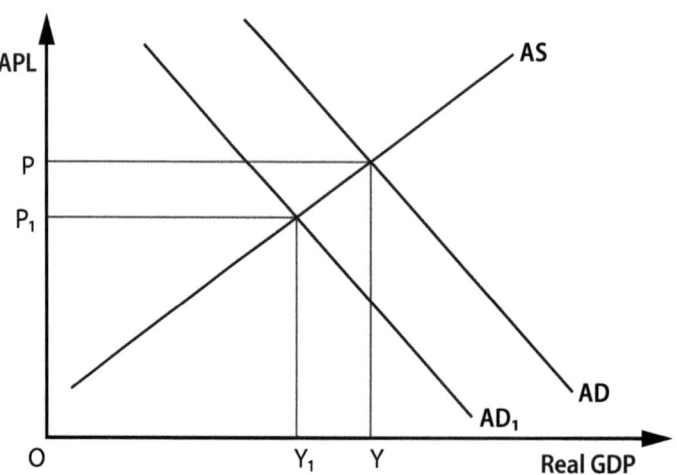

(e) The imposition of tariffs on imports of Turkish steel will lead to an increase in the price and a decrease in quantity imported as shown in the following diagram.

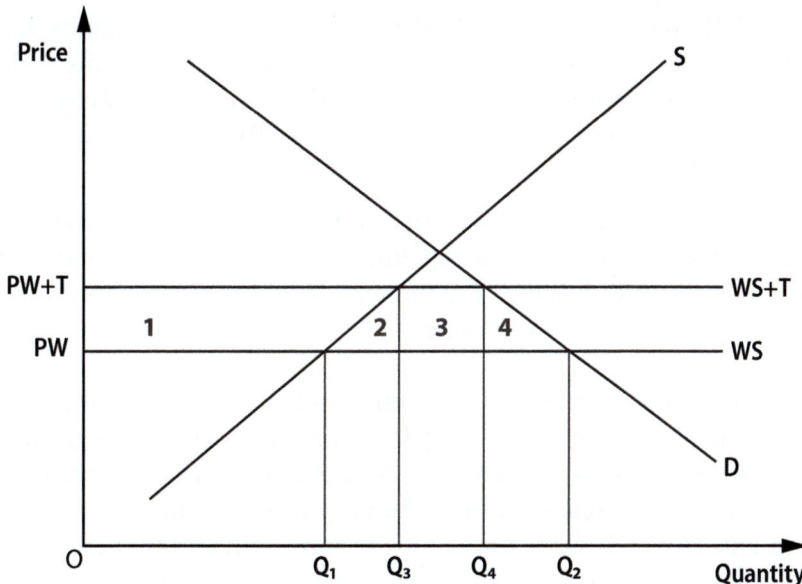

The price will increase to PW+T by the amount of the tariff and as a result the quantity imported will fall from $Q_1 - Q_2$ to $Q_3 - Q_4$.

(Note that for a different tariff related question we could also identify the loss of consumer surplus represented by the combined area 1+2+3+4. The revenue received by the government = area 3, the increase in producer surplus = area 1, the increase in domestic production = Q_1 to Q_3 and the deadweight loss = area 2 + 4).

(f) Both the increase in life expectancy and adult literacy will lead to an increase in the quality of the factor of production labour and as a result the PPC will shift outwards from PPC to PPC_1 as shown in the following diagram.

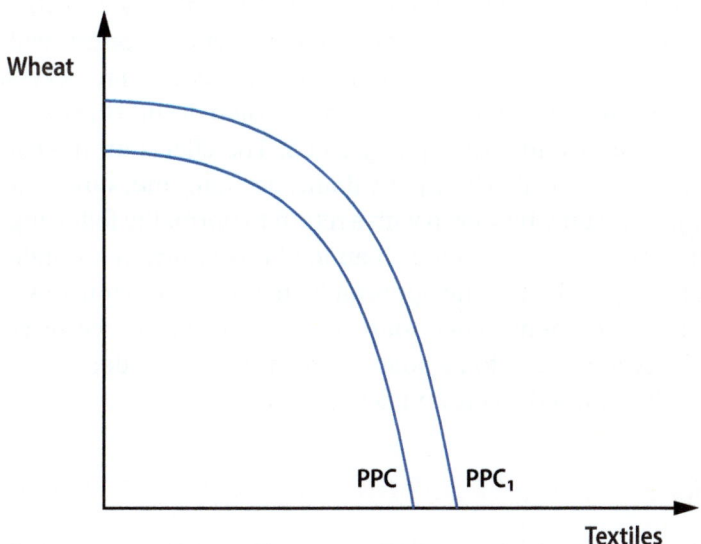

The improvements in health and literacy will lead to an increase in the productive potential of the Turkish economy.

(g) According to Text A paragraph 2, Turkey's current account deficit is problematically large at 3.4% of GDP and is mainly the result of the 20% drop in exports. The main reason for this appears to be the collapse of tourism identified in Text B caused by the Covid-19 travel restrictions. Unlike the dramatic fall in exports, imports have only fallen by 4% possibly because they constitute essential items such as oil and raw materials as opposed to less essential tourism. An additional contributory factor could be the trade restrictions through tariffs on Turkish steel exports imposed by the US described in Text C.

Faced with such a deficit a government has two main policy alternatives: expenditure switching and expenditure reducing, but in the current circumstances both policy approaches are problematic. Expenditure reducing policies are contractionary demand side policies which aim to shift AD to the left either by reducing government spending and/or increasing taxation (fiscal) or by increasing interest rates (monetary). These policies are only appropriate if the cause of the deficit is rising domestic demand which is resulting in more imports being bought. This however is not the case since as stated in Text B paragraph 3 the main cause of the deficit is the loss of export revenues from the huge drop in tourism as a result of travel restrictions. This is also a reason why expenditure switching policies would not work because making holidays in Turkey cheaper by reducing the exchange rate would not encourage more tourists because of the travel restrictions. In fact, as clearly shown in Table 1 the Turkish lira has depreciated significantly against the dollar already and any further depreciation would have no impact on exports which are down due to the pandemic. It would however lead to a higher rate of inflation which at 15.9% is already dangerously high. In addition, expenditure reducing policies would be extremely inappropriate given the dramatic fall in economic growth by 10% noted in Text A paragraph 1 combined with the drop in consumer demand from 7.2% to –1.4% according to Table 1. The current problem is not excess demand in the domestic economy, though this might have been a cause of pre 2019 deficits.

In view of these extraordinary circumstances, the current account deficit cannot be faced with traditional policies as they would only make the situation worse. What is required is a policy aimed at restoring confidence in the economy and the government's ability to bring the pandemic under control with an energetic vaccination program. Expansionary demand side policies are necessary to prevent the economy from descending further into recession despite the rising budget deficit indicated in Table 1 and Text A paragraph 3. The effects on the country's exports cannot be effectively dealt with by any domestic policy measures since the problem is external and will only be solved with a return to normality following a relaxation of travel restrictions. However, in anticipation of this return to normality in the future the government should take the opportunity to prepare the tourist sector for a more competitive environment. Since tourism is the major source of current account revenues the sector needs to be adapted to attract the modern visitor who is more technologically knowledgeable and demanding.

I selected this question in order to present an example of an untypical type of question where there is a unique situation that makes the normal approaches and solutions inappropriate. Since pandemic-based questions are likely to be around for some time it is important to be able to deal with them appropriately and within the context of traditional theory as required by the syllabus.

My suggestion when faced with such questions, as can be seen from the answer is to first outline what the normal policy approach would be and then to say why this would not be the best solution in the circumstances. If possible, some alternative suggestions should be offered and evaluated. Some references to diagrams that have been used in your answers to questions (c) to (f) could also be made and a variety of additional diagrams could be used to further show off your knowledge of economics, for example an exchange rate diagram showing the depreciation of the Turkish lira.

Question 3

Read the extracts and answer the questions that follow.

> ### Text A — Overview of China Trade Policy
>
> **US Congressman claims Chinese currency is still undervalued**
>
> (1) Despite the fact that China's current account surplus has fallen to below 3% of GDP, there are still complaints from the leader of the Democratic Trade Policy Group that China is giving its exports an artificial advantage by keeping the exchange rate of its currency, the Yuan, undervalued. He accused China of **dumping** and claimed that by manipulating its currency China is effectively subsidising its exports.
>
> (2) A Chinese trade spokesman replied that the US claims were exaggerated and pointed out that America was trying to blame others for its own internal and external imbalances and advised Congress to pursue domestic policies to redress these imbalances. He said that the Yuan has appreciated by 6% over the past year and that the US dollar was overvalued because of the continued weakness of the recovery in Europe combined with the European debt crisis which has depressed the value of the Euro.
>
> (3) A senior economist at the Economic Forum think-tank said that China's surplus looks set to fall further so its exchange rate is fairly close to true market value. He warned that China's internal imbalance was of greater concern with growth being driven by investment and exports rather than by domestic consumption. Without a healthy domestic demand stimulus China's economy is too exposed to the strength of the global recovery. If the EU recovery falters and the US fails to sustain its growth, China could face rising excess capacity and even a deficit on its current account.
>
> (4) A spokesman for a leading London investment bank said that an increase in oil and commodity prices could derail China's growth and add to its inflation problems. This could trigger labour unrest and demands for higher wages and cause an inflationary spiral to develop that would erode China's competitiveness in world markets.

Text B —US trade deficit better than it seems

(1) Many commentators have argued that the large US trade deficit is a sign that the American economy is losing its **comparative advantage** in manufacturing to lower cost producers in the, so called, BRIC economies. Even in the high-tech sector, countries like South Korea and China are gaining ground and seriously challenging America's dominant position, strengthening calls for increased trade protection.

(2) Closer examination of actual trade flows, however, reveal that many goods that appear as US imports are actually exports. The iPad is a good example of this. The total production cost of each iPad sold in America is roughly $275 and each one adds this amount to the recorded US deficit with China, which is where the iPad is manufactured. The total contribution to this amount by work carried out in China is about $10, which means that of the iPad import bill of $4 billion in 2011 only $150 million reflects actual value added by China. Approximately half the total value goes as profit, to the American owners, suppliers, designers and distributors. The same applies to many similar products which are US brands manufactured abroad.

(3) A leading economist at Chicago University has estimated that the real import content of the US deficit with China is about 50% of what the official statistics show. The main implication of this is that a revaluation of the Chinese currency would have a limited effect on the final import price of American brands imported from China. A 10% increase in the Yuan would add 0.5% to the import price of an iPad.

Text C — China claims top spot from US for new foreign investment

(1) Following a 50% decrease in investment by foreign firms in the US and a 4% increase in foreign direct investment (FDI) into China the world's second largest economy has now claimed the number one spot for new foreign investment.

(2) The reason for this is partly due to China's rapid recovery from the pandemic relative to that of the US as well as the policy followed by the Trump administration with trade restrictions that damaged America's reputation as a good place to do business.

Table 1: Economic Data for China

	2015 Data	2017 Data
Population (billions)	1.37	1.4 (2019)
GDP per capita (US$) (PPP)	14,800	16,600
GNI per capita (US$) at official exchange rate	8,740	7,940
Unemployment %	4	4
Inflation %	2.1	1.8
Gross National Savings (% GDP)	47.5	45.4
Exchange rate vs US$	6.23	7.76
GDP Growth Rate %	6.9	6,8

4. PAPER 2 PRACTICE QUESTIONS

Table 2: Development Data for China

	Previous Data	Later Data
Human Development Index (HDI)	0.739 (2015)	0.761 (2019)
Gini index	0.397 (2013)	0.385 (2016)
Life expectancy	75.9 (2015)	76.9 (2019)
Adult Literacy	92.71 (2010)	95.16 (2018)

Questions:

(a) (i) Define the term **dumping** indicated in bold (Text A, paragraph 1). [2 marks]

(ii) Define the term **comparative advantage** indicated in bold (Text B, paragraph 1). [2 marks]

(b) (i) Using information from Table 1, calculate the number of people unemployed in 2019 if the working population is 80% of the total population. [3 marks]

(ii) With reference to Table 1 explain the difference between GDP and GNI. [2 marks]

(c) Using an appropriate diagram explain the relevance of comparative advantage to international trade. (Text A, paragraph 1) [4 marks]

(d) Using an AD/AS diagram explain the effect of an increase in the US trade deficit on domestic output. (Text B, paragraph 1) [4 marks]

(e) Using an appropriate diagram, explain why export subsidies are an example of unfair trade. (Text A, paragraph 1) [4 marks]

(f) Using an appropriate diagram, explain how China might keep "the exchange rate of its currency, the Yuan, undervalued". (Table 2) [4 marks]

(g) Using information from the text/data and your knowledge of economics discuss the consequences of China allowing the value of the Yuan to appreciate and what policies it might implement to improve its development profile. [15 marks]

Answers

(a) (i) Dumping occurs when a country sells products in another country at prices that are below cost and is considered to be an example of unfair trade.

(ii) A country has comparative advantage in the production of a good when it can produce it at a lower opportunity cost than another country.

(b) (i) Unemployment = % of working population that is unemployed

Working population = 80% of 1.4 billion = 1.12 billion

Number unemployed = 4% of 1.12 billion = 44,800,000

(ii) GNI = GDP + Net property income from abroad

If GNI < GDP it means that outflows of property income are greater than inflows as is indicated by Table 1 (however, part of this actual difference is likely to be because the GDP is calculated at purchasing power parities while GNI is calculated at official exchange rates).

(c) Comparative Advantage

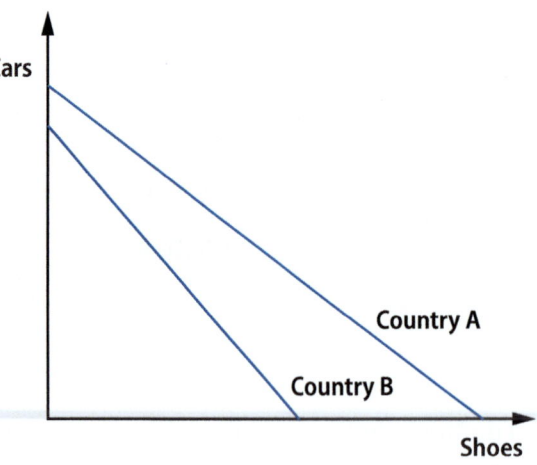

Comparative Advantage can be seen from the slope of the linear PPC but the easiest way of identifying it is simply to see the difference in production e.g. country A is more than twice as efficient in producing shoes but only a bit more efficient in producing cars.

Country A has an Absolute Advantage in the production of both shoes and cars (it is more efficient than country B in both goods). However, it is most efficient in producing shoes for which it has a lower opportunity cost while country B has a lower opportunity cost in the production of cars. Both countries will gain if A specialises in shoe production and B specialises in car production and engage in trade.

(d) An increase in the US trade deficit means that the value of net exports falls and since this is a component of AD, and other things being equal, there will be a decrease in the US AD as shown in the diagram below.

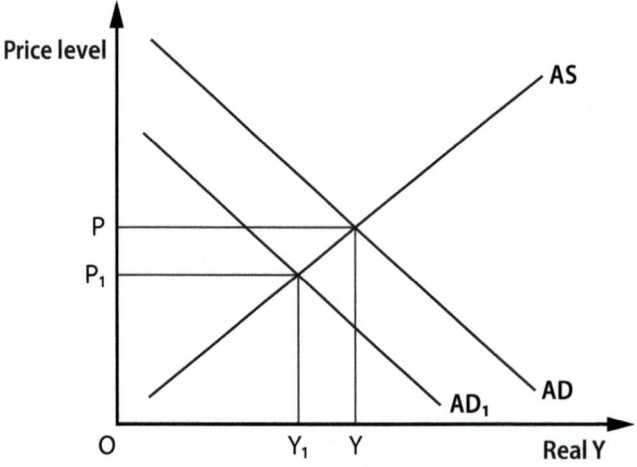

The shift in AD to AD_1 leads to a decrease in real output from Y to Y_1.

(e) Export subsidies give the exporters an unfair advantage because the subsidy artificially reduces their costs of production. The effect is shown in the following diagram where, as a result of the subsidy, the supply shifts to the right to S_s and the price is now lower at P_s. Whereas before the subsidy the export price was above the world price, after the subsidy it falls below the world price P_w and the exports may achieve an artificial comparative advantage. This is an unfair advantage and is regarded as a form of trade restriction or protectionism. It is a major source of dumping.

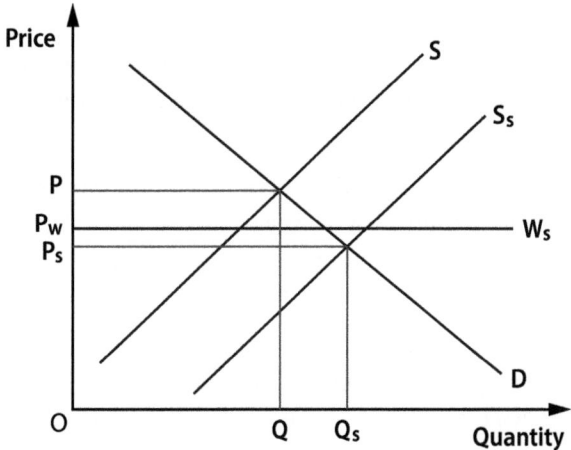

(f) The Chinese authorities can keep the exchange rate undervalued by intervening in the foreign exchange market as illustrated in the following diagram:

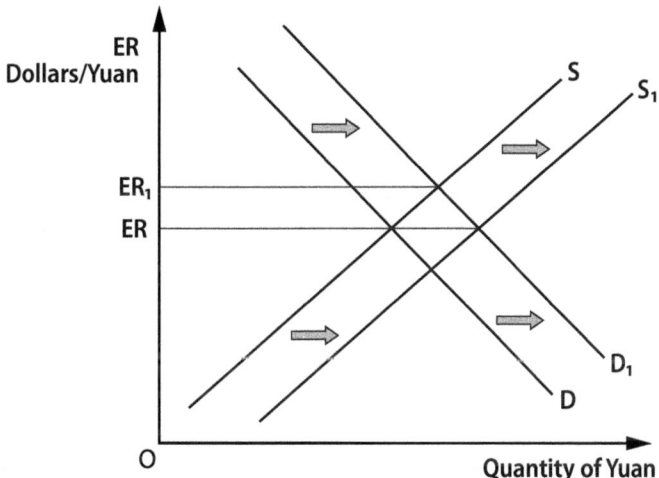

Because of China's surplus there is market pressure for the exchange rate to appreciate to ER_1, indicated by the shift in demand for the Yuan to D_1 from D. This reflects the increased demand for exports. To counteract this, the Chinese Central Bank will have to intervene in the market and sell Yuan, which is represented by the shift in supply to the right from S to S_1. As a result, the Yuan is kept at exchange rate ER.

(g) According to Text A paragraph 1, the undervalued currency gives China an unfair competitive advantage. Therefore, allowing the Yuan to appreciate would make China's exports less competitive and imports more competitive. The views expressed in Text A paragraph 2, however, imply that the Chinese currency is close to its market value and would not appreciate significantly, even if left to market forces. The problem seems to be more that the dollar is overvalued. This view is further supported in Text A paragraph 3.

Text A paragraph 4 also identifies the problem of inflation that China appears to be facing as a result of rising oil and commodity prices which could stimulate cost push inflation. This suggests that allowing the currency to appreciate could actually be good for China because it would help to bring down the cost of imported raw materials and help to keep down prices. In the long run, the reduction in import prices and production costs could neutralise the effect of higher export prices as a result of the exchange rate appreciation. Furthermore, exposing Chinese exporters to more competition as the exchange rate appreciates and makes exports more expensive, will force them to increase productivity, which is essential for sustained long term growth.

The effect of the appreciation on the current account surplus will depend on the relative elasticities of demand for China's exports and imports. If the Marshall-Lerner (M/L) condition is satisfied and combined elasticity of demand for exports and imports is > 1, then the surplus will decrease, but if the condition is not satisfied, the surplus will increase.

In the short run, the response of exports and imports to exchange rate changes is not very quick and the M/L condition is not easily met, in which case, the surplus will initially get larger. After about 6–9 months, however, it is expected that trade flows become more elastic so that the M/L condition will be met in the long run. This is shown in the following diagram which represents an inverted 'J' curve.

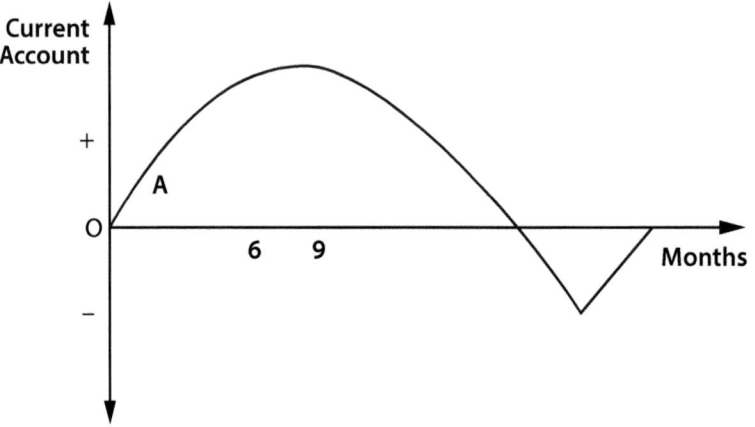

In the diagram above, it is assumed that the current account goes into surplus at point A. As a result, the exchange rate will appreciate, and this should restore current account balance because exports become more expensive, and imports become less expensive. However, in the short run, the (M/L) condition is not satisfied so the surplus becomes larger. In the long run, the condition will normally be met and the current account will eventually adjust and restore equilibrium.

In view of the dissatisfaction expressed by the US government in paragraph 1, allowing the currency to appreciate would alleviate these criticisms of dumping and could prevent the US from imposing protectionist policies which would be more damaging to Chinese exporters. This act of goodwill would promote good trade relations which would benefit both countries in the long run.

Allowing the currency to appreciate appears to be a sensible policy as it will establish better long term trade sustainability, and this is also likely to maintain the attractiveness of China for Foreign Direct Investment (FDI). As is noted in Text B, China has attracted many American companies such as Apple, which have set up production there. This high level of FDI has continued making China the top spot for such investment as stated in Text C. Such high levels of FDI are important in achieving development goals as well as promoting economic growth.

Despite the impressive growth rate of 6.8% and relatively low unemployment and inflation shown in Table 1, China's development profile is less impressive. Table 2 shows that in terms of life expectancy and adult literacy China is well below the average for the top developed economies which explains its relatively low HDI of 0.761. There is clearly scope for the government to invest more in health care and education which are key components of development, and this might also release some of the savings that are extremely high at over 45% of GDP. If there was more state provision of welfare and social services Families would not have to save so much and could consume more which would improve their development.

Question 4

Read the extracts and answer the questions that follow.

Text A — Overview of Brazil

(1) Brazil used to have one of the world's most unequal distributions of income and therefore a correspondingly high level of **relative poverty**, but over the past decade it has achieved the fastest reduction in inequality of any country. Between 2010 and 2019 poverty has fallen from 22 percent of the population to 7 percent and poor Brazilians have experienced income growth as much as seven times higher than that of rich Brazilians. This corresponds to high levels of growth of 6% for many years since 2000.

(2) The main credit for this remarkable achievement must go to the government and its conditional cash transfer (CCT) program. It is known as *Bolsa Familia* (Family Grant) in Brazil and involves the giving of cash to poor mothers on condition that their children attend schools and have vaccinations and that the mothers attend workshops about healthcare and nutrition.

(3) A similar scheme has been applied in Mexico where it is known as '*oportunidades*' with equal success and covers some 30% of the population. The cash transfers are relatively modest, but their regularity is enough to provide the incentive for families to meet the conditions. This not only lifts the families out of their current poverty but provides a source of long term development by raising the **HDI** as well as reducing the Gini coefficient.

(4) Even though inequality is falling in these countries, it tends to be rising in the developed countries of the world. The Gini coefficient for the USA is rising almost as quickly as Brazil's is falling so that it won't be long before income inequality is the same in both countries. This development casts some doubt on the claim that the free market is more successful in achieving social goals than government intervention.

(5) Critics of CCT programs argue that corruption will prevent the poor from receiving the cash and that the conditions are often unrealistic. In many poor countries there are simply not enough school places for the conditions to be met.

(6) CCT programs are by no means a perfect solution to global poverty, but they have had impressive results and are currently being applied in 40 countries. In all cases, there has been a marked improvement in health, nutrition, and educational achievement.

Text B — Brazil's economic growth poses a threat to global climate

(1) Growing world demand for meat products and cereals has given a boost to Brazil's agricultural sector as large-scale farming enterprises look to convert forest areas to pasture for grazing and the cultivation of crops.

(2) This has provided significant profits for the farmers and much needed export revenues for the country but has led to the most rapid rate of deforestation in over 20 years. The Amazon rainforest is crucial for the stability of the world's climate and this rate of destruction is likely to accelerate global warming.

(3) The Brazilian government denies these risks and maintains that the management of the rainforest is in accordance with sustainability requirements and that if other countries are so concerned, they should look to reforest their own pastureland.

(4) Some environmentalists are sympathetic with these views and claim that the developed countries should do more to shoulder the burden of climate change. Rather than blaming Brazil for increasing meat production they claim that the western consumer is more to blame by constantly increasing their demand for meat products.

Text C — Effects of US protectionist policies on China

(1) In retaliation to US tariffs on many Chinese products Beijing has announced the imposition of trade restrictions on imports of soya beans from the US. This has forced the American government to pay billions of dollars in compensation to soya bean farmers.

(1) As a result of these developments China has looked elsewhere for supplies of soya beans and Brazil has now become the major source of soya beans. In order to meet this increased demand, the pace of clearing forest areas to convert to arable farmland has accelerated in Brazil, posing additional threats to the sustainability of the rainforest.

(1) Environmental economists are divided regarding who is to blame with some blaming the climate change denial Brazilian President Bolsonaro while others blame the protectionist policies of the Trump administration.

Table 1: Economic Data for Brazil

	2017 Data	2019 Data
Population (millions)	207	210
GDP per capita (US$) (PPP)	10,250	12,647
GDP per capita (US$) at official exchange rate	8,827 (2015)	9,973 (2017)
Unemployment %	12.7	11.9
Inflation %	4.5	10.4
Gross National Savings (% GDP)	18.15 (2013)	12.54
Exchange rate vs US$	3.19	3.95
GDP Growth Rate %	1.3	1.1

4. PAPER 2 PRACTICE QUESTIONS

Table 2: Development Data for Brazil

	Previous Data (2017)	Later Data (2019)
Human Development Index (HDI)	0.761	0.765
Gini index	0.539 (2018)	0.534
Life expectancy	75.5	75.9
Adult Literacy	92.05 (2015)	93.23 (2018)

Questions:

(a) (i) Define the term **relative poverty** indicated in bold in Text A paragraph 1. [2 marks]

    (ii) Define the term **HDI** indicated in bold in Text A paragraph 3. [2 marks]

(b) (i) With reference to table 2 calculate the percentage change in adult literacy between 2015 and 2018. [2 marks]

    (ii) With reference to table 1 explain what is meant by GDP (PPP) [3 marks]

(c) Using an appropriate diagram explain the impact on Brazil's economy of the CCT programme (Text A paragraph 6) [4 marks]

(d) Using an appropriate diagram explain why increased demand for meat might generate a market failure. (Text B paragraph 2) [4 marks]

(e) Using an appropriate diagram explain the effect of the export revenues on the exchange rate of the Brazilian currency. (Text B paragraph 2) [4 marks]

(f) Using an appropriate diagram explain the impact on Brazil's economy of the change in savings indicated in Table 1. [4 marks]

(g) Using information from the text/data, and your knowledge of economics discuss the view that the costs of economic growth outweigh the benefits. [15 marks]

Answers:

(a) (i) Relative poverty is when a household's income is less than a certain percentage (usually 50%) of the average household income.

    (ii) HDI refers to the Human Development Index which is a composite measure that includes income, health and education (as measured by real GDP per head, life expectancy and adult literacy and school enrolment).

(b) (i) It has increased by 1.28% (Change/original × 100)

    (ii) GDP (PPP) refers to a measure of GDP converted to dollars at the purchasing power parity rather than the official exchange rate. PPP is considered to be a better indicator of the real value of a country's GDP because it shows what can be bought with a unit of currency.

(c) The CCT programme in Brazil is expected to lead to an increase in health, nutrition and education which will all contribute to an increase in the quality of the factor of production labour and as a result this will cause the long-run aggregate supply to shift from LRAS to $LRAS_1$ in the following diagram.

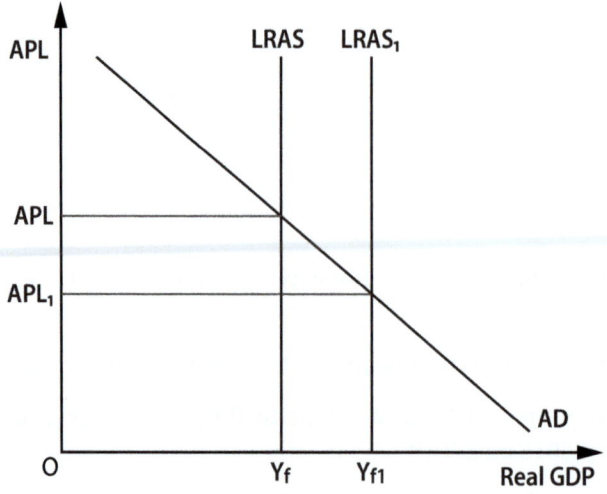

Note that the same result could be shown with a PPC diagram with a rightward shift in the PPC

The increase in LRAS will generate potential growth as the full employment level of income will increase to Y_{f1} and the average price level will fall to APL_1 thus reducing inflationary pressure.

(d) The increased demand for meat has led to an increase in meat production in Brazil which has involved some clearing of the rainforest, and this contributes to environmental degradation and climate change. These effects are costs to the whole global society and constitute negative production externalities. This leads to market failure and a welfare loss as shown in the following diagram.

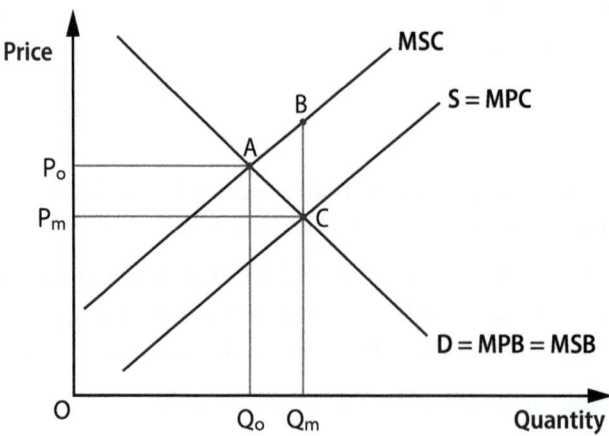

The market will establish price at P_m and output at Q_m which are determined by the interaction of supply, represented by the marginal private cost (MPC) and demand represented by the marginal private benefit (MPB) which is also equal to the marginal social benefit (MSB – assuming no consumption externality). The negative production externality means that the cost to society is higher than the private cost and is represented by the marginal social cost (MSC). The optimum situation for society is for price to be at P_o and the quantity to be at Q_o. There is therefore a market failure of over-production equal to $Q_m - Q_o$ leading to a welfare loss equal to ABC.

(e) Increased export revenues will, other things being equal, reflect an increased demand for the Brazilian currency from countries wanting to buy goods from Brazil and this will therefore have the effect of causing the exchange rate to appreciate as shown in the diagram below.

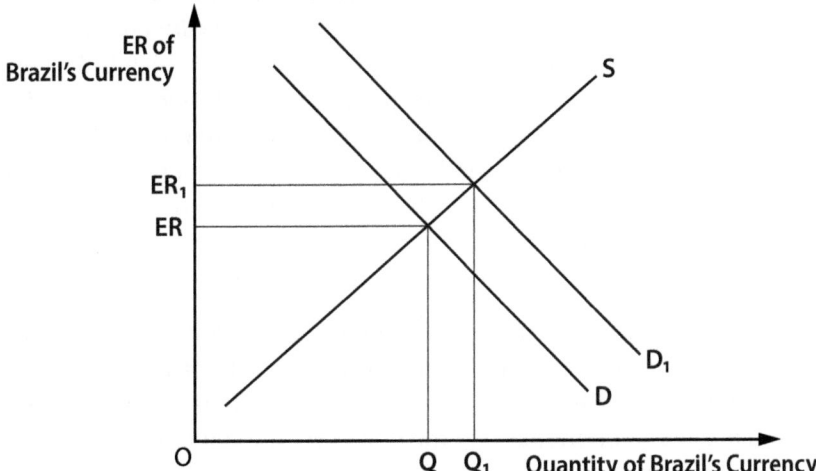

The demand increases from D to D_1 and as a result the exchange rate will increase from ER to ER_1.

(f) Gross national savings as shown in Table 1 have decreased from 18.15 to 12.54 as a % of GDP. This therefore corresponds to an increase in consumption spending which is a major component of aggregate demand. The diagram below shows the effect of this.

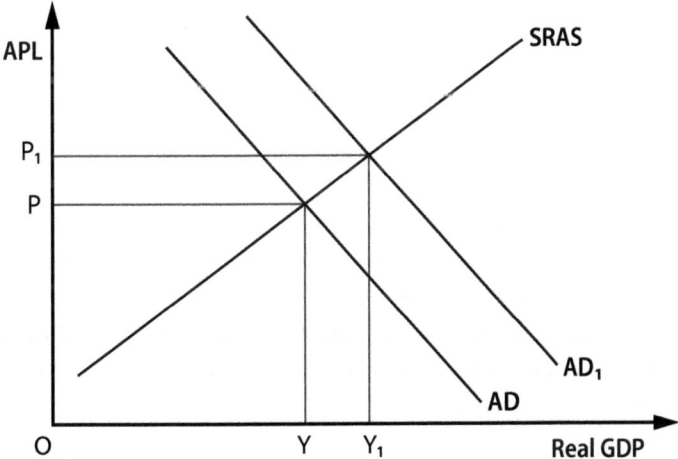

The increase in consumer spending causes AD to shift to the right to AD_1 and as a result there will be an increase in real GDP from Y to Y_1 and an increase in the average price level from P to P_1. (Note that the results could be different depending on whether we use a short-run AS, as I have, or a Keynesian AS or a neoclassical model).

(g) Economic growth is generally considered to be a desirable objective of government policy as it promotes a higher material standard of living and is also an important contributor to development through its ability to increase income. These links can be identified from the data in both Table 1 and Table 2. Brazil has enjoyed a relatively high growth rate of above 6% in the past but has slowed down recently. This increase in income has not been confined to the high-income groups since the Gini coefficient has decreased from 0.539 to 0.534 recently which indicates a slightly more equal distribution of income. In addition, the development indicators for Brazil have also improved with increases in HDI, adult literacy and life expectancy. These improvements are confirmed by the significant reduction in relative poverty identified in Text A paragraph 1. It is also likely that economic growth in Brazil has allowed for the government to engage in spending programmes such as the CCT which has clearly contributed to development as indicated in Text A.

All of these factors provide powerful evidence supporting the potential benefits of economic growth, however as Text B shows there are also costs involved which need to be considered. High levels of economic growth in developed and developing economies has led to an increase in the demand for meat and other income elastic products and this in turn has escalated the rate at which the Amazon rainforest is being converted to agricultural land. Exploiting the rainforest also contributes to Brazil's economic growth, but as pointed out in Text B it is also contributing to global warming which is a very urgent global problem and a threat to sustainability. Whether the increased income from economic growth is sufficient compensation for the environmental degradation that it creates is a difficult question, as is the location of responsibility. Is it the Brazilian farmers who are responsible or the consumers whose appetite for meat and cereals is driving the market?

Text C also poses this important question and indicates the trade conflicts between China and America which have their origin in China's recent economic growth which has led to the country becoming a serious challenge to American economic supremacy. It could be claimed that economic growth creates economic rivalry and that this is partly the cause of the trade conflict between China and the USA discussed in Text C, which in turn has further escalated the destruction of the rainforest.

Global warming and climate change are closely linked to the atmospheric pollution that has been created by the industrial production that has driven economic growth. The car is symbolic of the benefits of economic growth, but with increased car ownership has come traffic congestion and dangerously polluted urban centres. Are these car owners better off than their predecessors who lived in cleaner environments?

Economic growth can possibly provide the technological knowledge necessary to combat climate change together with the financial incentives and ability to tackle the problem of emissions with the development of cleaner substitutes. For example, with the replacement of petrol driven cars with electric vehicles and the development of green energy sources. However, in view of the threat posed to climate change and global warming from the destruction of the Amazon rainforest some more drastic action appears to be necessary, which might include changing consumption habits.

In the final analysis whether the costs of economic growth outweigh the benefits is a question that cannot be answered by positive economics as it involves a value judgement which is a normative economics issue.

4. PAPER 2 PRACTICE QUESTIONS

For this answer a variety of diagrams could have been used to illustrate points such as AD/AS to show growth or a Lorenz curve to show the change in income inequality, and references to diagrams used to answer questions (c) to (f) could also be used to enhance the answer.

It is *not* necessary to repeat diagrams used to answer previous questions and it is sufficient to refer back to them if you wish to include them.